THE HOME UNIVERSITY LIBRARY
OF MODERN KNOWLEDGE

234

ENGLISH PHILOSOPHY SINCE 1900

English Philosophy
since 1900

G. J. WARNOCK

LONDON
OXFORD UNIVERSITY PRESS
NEW YORK   TORONTO

Oxford University Press, Amen House, London E.C.4

GLASGOW NEW YORK TORONTO MELBOURNE WELLINGTON
BOMBAY CALCUTTA MADRAS KARACHI LAHORE DACCA
CAPE TOWN SALISBURY NAIROBI IBADAN ACCRA
KUALA LUMPUR HONG KONG

First edition May 1958
Reprinted 1959 *and* 1961

PRINTED IN GREAT BRITAIN

PREFACE

THIS book does not seek to make a contribution to philosophy. It is concerned with the contributions of others. Furthermore, since it deals with the present and the recent past, it can hardly aspire to the dignity of history.

It is certainly not a history of philosophy in general in this century, being confined almost entirely to the evolution of philosophy in this country. This restriction of scope, which it would have been tedious constantly to re-emphasize, should be kept carefully in mind. However, it appears to me to need no apology. For most philosophy written in English has been, for better or worse, and I shall not here say which, something vastly unlike most philosophy in other languages. This is not, as it is sometimes thought to be, a modern phenomenon. It has been broadly true for at least a century and a half, perhaps much longer. I do not know why. But the fact, whatever the explanation of it may be, makes it impossible to include both English and other philosophy within the compass of a book of this size, and would make it difficult to include both coherently in even a much longer account.

Another and more regrettable limitation consists in the fact that I have dealt with the work of rather few philosophers, to the total neglect of very much good work produced by very many others. I have done this for two reasons. In the first place, a commentary of this length must necessarily be selective. Its aim must be to make as clear as possible the general character of the philosophical landscape; and this requires concentration on those philosophers whose work has bulked large, has been influential on others, or has been representative of some sort of general view, position, theory, or trend. A philosophical book or article may well be of great merit and interest, without being well-adapted for this purpose of illustrating general tendencies and positions. There are many books and articles of that sort which are nowhere mentioned in the following pages; and I hope that, with this explanation, their authors will not construe their neglect for my present purpose as a sign of disrespect. In any case, great philosophers of conspicuous influence are not by any means always very good philosophers. In this field as in many others, the great and the good are quite often not the same people.

My second reason for being highly selective is perhaps more contentious. I have tried to pick out what seemed to me most important in recent and contemporary philosophy, and to deal with this in reasonable detail; by contrast I have ignored altogether such elements of unorthodoxy and dissent as were, in my judgement, of no permanent significance. Such judgement is fallible, and certainly always disputable. Readers who may not be very familiar with what might be called the politics of contemporary philosophy can, I believe, be fairly assured that the sketch of the landscape given here is not an eccentric one; but they are also entitled to the warning that there are some philosophers, and doubtless many non-philosophers, who would regard the account which follows as odiously partisan. This charge might have been evaded by some kind of encyclopaedic neutrality; but I believe it is better that it should be boldly incurred.

It will be noticed that I have given no special attention to moral or political philosophy. This is explained partly by limitation of space, and partly by the belief that those subjects—at least as they are currently pursued—do not differ in any point of principle from philosophical inquiries in general, and hence do not really call for a separate commentary. I hope that this omission will not be taken to suggest either disrespect for the valuable work in this field that has recently been done, or the idea that there is no other kind of work that could be done. Either of these suggestions would be quite out of place.

The fact that I have said nothing about recent work in the history of philosophy is easily accounted for by the fact that the history of philosophy, though certainly it is not just history, is not just philosophy either, and hence is for the most part only indirectly or incidentally relevant to the course of philosophy itself.

One word more of explanation is necessary. There has recently appeared quite a number of general surveys of 'contemporary' philosophy, and I have been partly concerned to avoid too much treading over the very same ground. For this reason I have given a good deal of space to very recent philosophy indeed, at the expense of the earlier years of the present century. It is probably true that a really just account can be given only of what is comparatively distant in time, and probably for this good reason most recent commentators have dealt much more fully with the philosophy of some years ago than with that of the present. It seemed worth attempting, however, to redress this balance of emphasis. The first part of this book, then, has been deliberately compressed. It may be that the consequent distortion has amounted, in certain cases, almost to caricature; if so, I hope that this will not be thought unpardonable. In some ways the chief sufferer from the policy of compression has been, I think, Logical Atomism; and here my particular reason has been that Logical Atomism was the main subject of Professor Urmson's admirable book *Philosophical Analysis*.[1]

It goes without saying, of course, that compression and simplification in some degree have been necessary everywhere. But fortunately no reader of this book need have much difficulty in checking against the original documents the account of the state of philosophy that is here submitted. A rather oppressive awareness of the imperfections of that account has led me to include at the end of the text a list of some relevant articles and books, to which readers of the pages that follow are most earnestly referred.

[1] Oxford University Press, 1956.

CONTENTS

NOTE TO THIRD IMPRESSION

SINCE this book was first published two of the most influential philosophers discussed in it have died— G. E. Moore in October 1958, J. L. Austin in February 1960. Austin, who was only forty-eight when he died, had published comparatively little; the loss to philosophy in England cannot be made good, but three posthumous volumes will be issued shortly by the Clarendon Press, two of which will consist wholly of material not previously published.

June, 1961.   G. J. W.

Chapter I

THE POINT OF DEPARTURE

IN 1924 and 1925 there appeared two bulky volumes with the general title *Contemporary British Philosophy*. They make strange reading today. Their title itself, even then, was doubtfully appropriate. For the philosophical landscape which, in their own odd way, these books illuminate is that of a period some years earlier than their dates of publication. The essays of which they consist were written for the most part by philosophers who were already veterans, and the few contributions by younger men stand out most awkwardly among their venerable companions. The editor of the two volumes, J. H. Muirhead, expressed his belief that British philosophy had been brought back 'into the main stream of European thought', and added the hope that 'the present generation' would remain and prosper in that stream as he conceived it.[1] This hope, as the work of his younger contributors might well have led him to suspect, was doomed to almost immediate extinction. It might have seemed reasonable enough in, say, 1900; but it should have been clear by 1925 that the scene had changed, was changing, and would continue to change.

This transformation, though its early stages appear to have eluded the notice of Muirhead, has become by now a sufficiently conspicuous fact. It has been often

[1] op. cit., First Series, p. 323.

remarked upon, sometimes with satisfaction, sometimes with lamentation and dismay. It has almost as often been misunderstood. It has been said to have generated a kind of 'revolutionary illusion', through which neither its friends nor its enemies can see the case clearly. It stands, in fact, in need of explanation. To attempt to explain exhaustively *why* there occurred the changes that did occur would be an enterprise both ill-defined and, for the present at least, over-ambitious; but it ought to be possible to make at least reasonably clear what sort of transformation it is that we have to deal with.

Over Muirhead's two volumes of 'contemporary' British philosophy there broods the conspicuous presence of F. H. Bradley. Bradley was at that time too old to be represented in them in his own person. But he is mentioned in the preface as 'by general acknowledgement the foremost figure in British philosophy (perhaps in the philosophy of our time in any country) for the last generation'; and indeed very many of the essays that follow bear the marks of his doctrines, of his manner of thought, and of his style of writing. Another large presence is that of Bernard Bosanquet. Of these two H. J. Paton has recently written[1] that 'in their day and generation they were big men'; for philosophers generally they were 'the dominant figures even to those who opposed them'. The dominant doctrine which these big men represented, and which formed for many years the pervasive

[1] *Contemporary British Philosophy*, Third Series, Allen and Unwin, Macmillan, 1956, p. 343.

atmosphere of philosophy, has been called Absolute Idealism—in Paton's words, 'Hegelianism modified by Anglo-Saxon caution'. It was almost inevitable that philosophers of that period, even those of whom it would now seem difficult to believe, at some stage or other should all have thought of themselves as Hegelians of this modified variety. The chief architects of change, Bertrand Russell and G. E. Moore, though the stage in their cases was decidedly a brief one, were not exceptions to the general rule.

It would be extremely difficult to say what this species of philosophy exactly was. Perhaps indeed it was nothing at all exactly. It will be enough to say here in broad terms what it was like. It was in the first place highly and ambitiously metaphysical. The claim was made, that is, to establish striking and important conclusions about the universe as a whole, about Reality, not in this or that more or less superficial or limited aspect, but in its ultimate nature. The philosopher's concern with 'the whole' was constantly and powerfully contrasted with the merely partial or fragmentary interests of other disciplines; his endeavour to arrive at really 'ultimate' truths was distinguished from, say, scientific attempts to establish propositions that would serve for some non-ultimate purpose, or would satisfy some more or less arbitrary or provisional standard. It was held that what passed for truths in the world, or in the laboratory, were all, or almost all, somehow unsatisfactory—that for the philosopher there was not only something more, but also something very different, to be said.

The motives underlying these high endeavours were various, and not always explicitly avowed. It appears that Bradley was impelled by a dissatisfaction, which he himself half admitted to be not wholly intellectual, with all common and current ways of thinking and speaking. His discontent was a very fundamental one. We are all inclined to take it for granted, whatever our special interests, if any, may be, that the universe contains or consists of a number of things—that this unremarkable and rather un-informative proposition is surely as true as anything could be. But it appears to have been just this proposition which Bradley detested. It seemed to him to carry with it a view of the universe as a mere plurality of items; as fragmentary, disjointed, and irrational; as infected throughout with what most displeased him—namely 'bare conjunction'. It seemed to him that 'reason' could not tolerate such a view of the universe as this. He therefore set himself to show, with vast and indeed valuable ingenuity, that everything which, on this fundamental assumption, is taken to be real or true is, in an odd sense of his own, self-contradictory—is therefore to be condemned as 'mere appearance', as quite alien to the ultimate nature of Reality. Reality is to be found only in the Absolute, which neither is nor contains a number of things; in which all separation is overcome, all distinctions vanish, all seeming individuals and their apparent relations are merged; in which, in short, there remains no hint of any bare conjunction.

The motives of Bosanquet were in part rather different from this. He shared with Bradley the conviction that only the Absolute, 'the whole', was entirely satisfactory; he shared his small regard for ordinary ways of thinking. But he was influenced also, as Bradley was not much, by the hope of discovering some ultimate, unshakeable basis for ethics, or more generally some sort of guarantee for all judgements of value. If, he explained, we 'experience the positive quality of the absolute', then 'the intrinsic connexion of reality and value becomes here transparent to us'.[1] We see that 'totality expresses itself in value'. J. E. McTaggart, a rather younger Cambridge philosopher who zealously shared in the general deference to Hegel, was even more candid as to his practical interest. 'The utility of Metaphysics is to be found', he said, 'in the comfort it can give us'—'in the chance that it may answer this supreme question (whether good or evil predominates in the universe) in a cheerful manner, that it may provide some solution which shall be a consolation and an encouragement.'[2] However, whereas Bosanquet and many of his contemporaries were inclined to the view that philosophy might sometimes justify and even demand positive social or political action, McTaggart seems rather to have thought that 'comfort' was enough. If we found that the universe was a fairly cheerful place, there was not much that we could do to make it more cheerful still.

It is not surprising that a philosophy of this variety—so ambitious, so deliberately un-ordinary, so determinedly grave—should have found expression in a

[1] *Contemporary British Philosophy, First Series*, p. 72.

[2] *Philosophical Studies*, pp. 184, 151.

characteristic manner of writing; and indeed it is
probably the change in this respect which would strike
most immediately a reader who compared the philosophy of fifty years ago with that of today. If he were
attached to the presently prevailing mode, and had the
courage of his convictions, he might well find the style
of the Idealists almost unbearable. It had at its best an
undeniable splendour. Bradley in particular was
capable of impressive rhetoric, and conveys quite
often in his extraordinary sentences a sense of ex-
plosive intellectual energy. Bosanquet's manner was
less idiosyncratic but more literary than Bradley's, and
closer to bombast. He wrote sometimes with an air
of vague high seriousness, in which the serious intent
was almost completely muffled by the vagueness. And
in the writings of the lesser men solemnity and unclarity seem to rise not seldom to the pitch of actual
fraud. But it is necessary to be careful in framing, if
one wishes to frame, a complaint about this state of
affairs. It might seem the merest truism to say that, if
argument is to be carried on, rhetorical figures, stylistic
variation, and literary high colour can only be distress-
ing impediments: and it was precisely on his superior
logical acumen and argumentative rigour that the
Idealist metaphysician was most apt to insist. If so,
it might seem reasonable to object that his prose was a
medium most ill-suited to the display of his talents;
inflation of language is almost always irritating, but it
positively frustrates the close exposition of an argument. However, it may be that this objection would be
mis-placed. It may be, as Bradley would presumably

have wished it to be, that there was an 'intrinsic' and not merely fortuitous relation between Idealist thought and the usual style of its expression. Bradley's opinions perhaps, whatever his claims may have been, were not strictly susceptible of demonstration, but depended, among the relatively unimportant trappings of argument, mainly upon the persuasive force and artifice of their presentation. If so, to strip off the highly coloured rhetorical dress would be to harm substantially the doctrine itself, or even to find that one arrived, as with an onion, at nothing in the end. The Idealists could hardly have been expected to do this for themselves.

The movement of philosophy away from this prevailing atmosphere has often been represented, usually by hostile critics, as a break with tradition. We are sometimes told not only that British (or English-speaking) philosophy of the recent past is not what philosophy used to be, which no doubt is to be expected, but that it is something of a quite different sort from what it had been by long tradition; it is implied that this must merit concern or even dismay. In this idea there is, as we shall find, not no truth at all, but there is in it also a measure of historical falsehood. It is true that philosophy in the manner of Bosanquet and Bradley has, in defiance of the forecasts of J. H. Muirhead, declined to a condition very nearly approaching nonexistence; but it is not true that philosophy in that manner was ever, in this country, the usual or traditional thing. On the contrary, the state of British philosophy in the early years of the present century

B

'mainstream'

was itself highly unusual and full of novelty. It bred, no doubt, its own revolutionary illusions. To see in it now a tradition is certainly a mistake. It may possibly have been, as Muirhead twenty years later thought that it still was, in 'the main stream of European thought'. But it is unquestionable that it had not been there for very long, and that the main stream of *British* thought had run for some centuries in very different channels.

This was clear enough to a foreign observer. The Italian De Ruggiero, whose *Modern Philosophy* was published in 1912, was of the opinion that 'the speculative level reached by English Idealism' was high. But he saw clearly that this then dominant mode of thought was still very new in British philosophy, and he confessed himself unable to explain how his British contemporaries had done, as he thought, so well in so short a time. He suggested some connexion with the Romantic revival. He mentioned the names of Coleridge, Wordsworth, Carlyle, and Ruskin. He alluded to the stimulus of late Victorian agnosticism, so exasperating to 'a religious race like the English'. But the start of the strictly philosophical movement could be dated exactly, he held, from the publication in 1865 of J. H. Stirling's *The Secret of Hegel*. There is indeed much evidence to suggest that it was in fact at about this time that 'German Idealism began to find a home in British universities'. English and Scottish philosophers may have started late in this particular race, but their fervour very rapidly made up for their comparative tardiness. It has been said that they expressed 'the vital spirit of an era'. If an era may be measured in intensity and not only in duration, the remark is not quite wholly absurd.

However, it is clearly very far from being the case that the brand of philosophy from which reaction was so soon to occur was in England time-hallowed and venerably traditional. It was in fact an exotic in the English scene, the product of a quite recent revolution in ways of thought due primarily to German influences. Bertrand Russell, a major cause of the exotic's demise, was the god-son of John Stuart Mill, 'so far as is possible in a non-religious sense',[1] and he thus symbolically joins hands with at least two centuries of British philosophy, across a gap of a few years occupied with new and strange things. Of course, the fact that Absolute Idealism was a recent and very much an alien import does not entail that it deserved the extinction which overtook it. But to think of it as *traditional* is to imply on its behalf a claim to respect to which it is not entitled. Conversely, to regard Moore and Russell merely as innovators is to forget that there exists, far removed from what they opposed, another lengthy tradition with which they are quite firmly connected. Hume or Berkeley would have been sadly puzzled by the pages of Bradley, to say nothing of Hegel's. But either might have conversed quite naturally with Moore, and with Russell too, at least in his less technical moments.

Nor should the extent of the reaction led by Russell and Moore be exaggerated. They were not at first, and perhaps have never been, opposed in general to

[1] *The Philosophy of Bertrand Russell*, p. 3.

metaphysics. Moore said in 1910 that 'the most important and interesting thing which philosophers have tried to do' is to give 'a general description of the *whole* of the Universe';[1] and this, the characteristic metaphysical aim, he certainly did not consider to be in principle vicious or impossible. Russell announced in 1918 his own intention of setting forth 'a certain kind of metaphysic',[2] and he believed that this could be attempted with good prospects of success. He intended to replace Absolute Idealism with a *different* system of metaphysics; while Moore, who had no system of his own, was for the most part engrossed in trying to establish to his own satisfaction the meaning of, and the grounds for, the many surprising things which Idealist and other philosophers had said. He did not think they had said nothing, or that what they had said could not possibly be true. The idea that metaphysics is in principle impossible, or 'meaningless', did not appear until many years later, at a time when, in this country at least, old-style Idealism was already moribund; and even then, it was an idea which neither Russell nor Moore either sponsored or accepted.

It would also, I believe, be historically improper to give the impression that Idealism perished of *refutation*. It is true that some of Bradley's fundamental views, such as his doctrine of 'internal relations' or his theory of truth, were subjected to destructive criticism. But metaphysical systems do not yield, as a rule, to

[1] *Some Main Problems of Philosophy*, p. 1.

[2] *The Philosophy of Logical Atomism*: see *Logic and Knowledge*, ed. Marsh, 1956, p. 178.

frontal attack. Their odd property of being demonstrable only, so to speak, from within confers on them also a high resistance to attack from outside. The onslaughts of critics to whom, as likely as not, their strange tenets are very nearly unintelligible are apt to seem, to those entrenched inside, mis-directed or irrelevant. Such systems are more vulnerable to *ennui* than to disproof. They are citadels, much shot at perhaps but never taken by storm, which are quietly discovered one day to be no longer inhabited. The way in which an influential philosopher may undermine the empire of his predecessors consists, one may say, chiefly in his providing his contemporaries with other interests. In the present case the old spells were broken, and a new spell was cast, chiefly by reason of the character of G. E. Moore.

Chapter II

G. E. MOORE

I HAVE just indicated that, among the immediately operative factors contributing to the decay of Absolute Idealism, special notice should be paid to the *character* of Moore. The word may have seemed, perhaps, curiously chosen; but it was chosen deliberately. For it was not solely by reason of his intellectual gifts that Moore differed so greatly from his immediate predecessors, or influenced so powerfully his own contemporaries. He was not, and never had the least idea that he was, a much cleverer man than McTaggart, for example, or Bradley. It was in point of character that he was different, and importantly so. He seems to have been, in the first place, entirely without any of the motives that tend to make a metaphysician. He was neither discontented with nor puzzled by the ordinary beliefs of plain men and plain scientists. He had no leanings whatever towards paradox and peculiarity of opinion. He had no particular religious or other cosmic anxieties; and he seems to have felt that in aesthetics and morality (not, of course, in moral or aesthetic *philosophy*) all was as well, at least, as could reasonably be expected. He thus did not hanker for any system on his own account. But secondly, he had the great force of character that was necessary to resist the temptation to conform himself with his environment. He soon overcame, if he ever had, the

desire so natural in any clever young man, to excel in
the same line of business as his admired elders. He
did not borrow a modish metaphysical idiom to make
up for, or to conceal, his own real lack of relish for any
such thing. And thirdly, he seems never to have had
the slightest difficulty in causing his views to be taken
seriously. It was always clear that his opinions, however unorthodox or naïve they may have been or
seemed, were not those of one who could safely be
disregarded.

The character of his original interest in philosophy
was both very simple and, in its context, strikingly
original. He went to Cambridge in 1892 to read
classics, hardly aware at that time 'that there was such a
subject as philosophy'. But the encouragement of,
among others, Bertrand Russell first engaged his
interest in philosophical discussions, and then led him,
at the end of his first year, to start reading philosophy.
His concern with the subject was, in a sense, indirect.
'I do not think that the world or the sciences would ever
have suggested to me any philosophical problems. What
has suggested philosophical problems to me is things
which other philosophers have said about the world or
the sciences.'[1] In discussions at Cambridge he
heard propositions asserted to which he could attach
no clear meaning, and he sought to have it explained
what their meaning was. He heard things asserted
which he could see no sufficient reason to believe, and
he tried to find out on what grounds the assertions were

---

[1] *The Philosophy of G. E. Moore*, p. 14.

made. It appeared to him that his companions sometimes denied what every sane man knew quite well to
be true, and he made patient efforts to persuade them
that they ought not to do this. McTaggart on one
occasion 'had been led to express his well-known view
that Time is unreal. This must have seemed to me
then (as it still does) a perfectly monstrous proposition,
and I did my best to argue against it. I don't suppose I
argued at all well; but I think I was persistent.'[1] No
doubt he was.

The most striking feature of his philosophical
questioning was, perhaps, its very simplicity and
directness. His mind has always worked most naturally
in concrete terms. If Time is unreal, ought we not to
deny that we have breakfast *before* we have lunch?
If Reality is spiritual, does it not follow that 'chairs and
tables are far more like us than we think'? Can it
really be doubtful whether material objects exist,
since it is certain that here is one hand and here is
another? Moore did not in every case wish to suggest
that the strange things philosophers said were certainly
untrue. But he did wish to make it quite plain that
they were very strange. He wished to point out how
astonishing were their implications. He wanted to
have it understood how much work was to be done, if
grounds were to be offered that would really require
their acceptance. In all of this he was neither obstinate
nor disingenuous. He was not less well able to follow
an intricate argument than were the philosophers he
questioned; he was far more exacting in his standards

[1] *The Philosophy of G. E. Moore*, p. 14.

of clarity and rigour. His puzzlement, indeed his
bewilderment, at the things they were willing to assert
was entirely sincere. He was gradually driven to the
disturbing conclusion that an enormous amount of
philosophical writing was marred and frustrated by
hastiness and *confusion*. Philosophers, it seemed to him,
were fatally addicted to embarking on the search for
answers to important-seeming questions without
considering *exactly* what questions they were trying to
answer. They were liable, too, to make one or two
points in an argument, and forthwith to consider their
whole question as closed. But often, even usually,
these points could be shown to be, however impeccable
in themselves, entirely inadequate as grounds for the
conclusion supposedly based on them. If the conclusion was, as conclusions were by no means always,
clear, it might be obvious enough that the question
whether it was true or false was exceedingly interesting.
'Reality', for example, 'may be spiritual, for all I know;
and I devoutly hope it is.' That opinion at least is
'truly interesting and important'. But one must
realize how very *different* the opinion is from what
any ordinary person believes; how *many* propositions
must be disproved and proved, before it could possibly
be said to be established; what a vast number of
arguments must, therefore, be involved; and how
remote we are, really, from any position in which we
would see the doctrine to be true or, alternatively,
false. The usual starting-point for Moore's early
work was something which seemed to him to be, if not
a 'perfectly monstrous proposition', at least a very

strange and surprising proposition; and his 'method', if indeed he can be said to have had any such thing, was simply to raise, with regard to its meaning and its grounds, any question he could think of that seemed to him to be in need of an answer. He found that such questions were numerous enough to provide him with plenty of hard work.

The effect, in the highly elaborated and refined atmosphere of Idealism in the 1890s, of the appearance of such a simple, direct, pertinacious inquirer can easily be imagined. It was supposedly agreed on all hands that quite ordinary opinions were quite certainly defective; that common ways of speaking were almost always unsatisfactory; and that *therefore* it was quite clearly imperative to devise new ways of speaking, new and subtler opinions, in order to withstand the close scrutiny of philosophical criticism. There was doubtless no agreement as to what particular refinements were called for, or exactly what paradoxes they were that should be boldly embraced; but there was no disposition to question the general view that very many very common opinions must be ruthlessly rejected. Moore struck in fact, though perhaps unwittingly, at the very foundations of all the current philosophical structures. He asked, in effect, why they were *needed*. What exactly was supposed to be wrong with very ordinary opinions? Why exactly were common ways of speaking to be condemned? So far from being disposed to assume that beliefs very widely held were very probably mistaken, he was inclined to suppose that they were almost certain to be true. If not, exactly why not? And if some other opinion were put forward as being an improvement, what was it exactly, and how was it thought to be established? For some people at least, the mere raising of such questions as these—the mere refusal to submit without question to Idealist spells—had apparently the force of a liberation. The emperor was seen to have, if not quite no clothes, at least not very many. Russell himself has said that Moore's influence worked upon him as an 'emancipation';[1] it proved possible to walk out of the intellectual prison as soon as a simple, open-eyed inspection was made of its walls. Why should one try to believe that Time is not real? There was quite suddenly seen to be no reason at all.

What then, if one abandoned the aim of constructing paradoxical alleged improvements upon, or corrections of, people's ordinary opinions, was left for the philosopher to do? There remained, of course, the considerable task of unravelling the pronouncements of other philosophers; and to this Moore himself devoted a great deal of attention. But he did not think, or at least did not think for very long, that this was the only sort of task for philosophers to undertake. There was also the task which he called 'analysis'. Here we must turn to some actual examples.

In 1925 Moore published an article called 'A Defence of Common Sense'.[2] It begins with a list of what he calls 'truisms'—such as that he has a body,

[1] *The Philosophy of Bertrand Russell*, p. 12.

[2] *Contemporary British Philosophy*, Second Series, pp. 193-223.

was born a certain number of years ago, has lived since that time on or near the surface of the earth, which itself had existed for many years before he was born, and on which live and have lived very many other human beings. Every one of these propositions, Moore says, 'I *know*, with certainty, to be true'. They are all *wholly* true; their meaning is in no way doubtful or obscure; and Moore knows also that very many other people know vastly many truths of a sort similar to these. However, he observes that a great many philosophers have made assertions apparently incompatible with these truisms. They have asserted that there are no material things at all, that Time is unreal, that perhaps there exist no minds other than their own; and in some cases at least, Moore believes, they have used such words as these in such a way as really to contradict some or all of his truisms. At the same time, it is quite certain that they knew those truisms to be true. For even in their philosophical writings they have alluded to themselves, and to other philosophers, or to possible readers, in such a way as to reveal their knowledge of the existence of themselves and of other people, and of the ordinary world in which they and others were living. The chief peculiarity of Moore's own position is, he says, that while he shares with all other philosophers the knowledge that what may be called 'the Common Sense view of the world' is, in certain fundamental respects, wholly true, he does not *also* hold, as they have often done, views inconsistent with that view of the world. 'But this difference seems to me to be an important one.'

But, he goes on to say, he does not mean to imply that there are no questions for serious dispute. For although, with regard to all his truisms, it would be 'quite certainly the height of absurdity' to wonder whether they are true, or whether we know this, it is no less certainly quite proper to wonder what is the correct *analysis* of them. Indeed, 'no philosopher, hitherto, has succeeded in suggesting an analysis of them, as regards certain important points, which comes anywhere near to being certainly true'. It is not, as some philosophers appear to have thought, that their analysis is clear but their truth uncertain. The case is exactly the reverse of this. Their truth is absolutely certain, but their analysis is doubtful.

Some years later, in 1939, Moore discussed[1] the observation of Kant that, if anyone expresses doubt of the existence of 'things outside us', 'we are unable to counter his doubts by any satisfactory proof'. Moore first examines with very great care the meaning of the expression 'things outside us'. He decides that, though there may be some things as to which it is doubtful whether they should be so called, yet there are very many things that would, if they existed, certainly be of the kind in question—as for instance dogs, planets, stars, shadows, and hands. He then offers a proof that there do exist things outside us. 'Here is one hand', he says, 'and here is another'; therefore, at least two things outside us exist; and one could add as many other such proofs as might be required. The premises

[1] *Proof of an External World*, Hertz Annual Philosophical Lecture. London, Humphrey Milford.

here are quite certainly true, and the conclusion quite certainly follows from the premises. There is no doubt, he says, that the proof is 'perfectly conclusive'. Once again, however, he is careful to make the admission that the *analysis*, both of the premises and the conclusion, is more than doubtful. It is proper to wonder how such propositions ought to be analysed; the absurdity consists only in wondering whether they are true, in supposing that they are not known, or that they cannot be proved.

Before raising the question what Moore means here by 'analysis', we ought to take notice of the baffled astonishment which both of these papers are liable to generate. Are they not, one is tempted to protest, altogether too simple? Can it really be that many philosophers have held opinions rather obviously incompatible with what they themselves and others knew to be true? Can it be that Kant did not know that he had two hands, or did not see that hands fell under the heading of 'things outside us'? Can it really be to the point to insist that certain propositions are true, which are in fact just what Moore calls them—that is, truisms? Surely there must be more to it than this. But what more?

Attempts have been made to bring out the point of Moore's procedure, and hence to remove the sense of baffled astonishment, by supposing that he slightly misstated his case. It has been suggested[1] that he was

[1] e.g. by Malcolm, in *The Philosophy of G. E. Moore*, pp. 345-68. Malcolm has subsequently retracted some points in his argument.

really concerned with the defence, not of Common Sense, but of *ordinary language*. Suppose it to be agreed, as it naturally would be, that there frequently arise situations in which, if someone were to say 'This is a hand', it would by all ordinary standards, and taking the words in their ordinary sense, be admitted that what he said was true, and that he knew what he said was true. Now it might perhaps be urged that there are other standards, and other senses of the words, according to which what he said was *not* true, or at least he did not know it to be true; and some philosophers might wish to maintain that these other standards and senses were *correct*, in opposition to those that we all ordinarily employ. Moore's point, on this interpretation, would then be that it does not make sense, when discussing an expression in ordinary language, to argue thus that its ordinary employment is *not correct*. For what could be the correct way of employing it, if not the way in which it is ordinarily employed by those who know the language in question? Moreover, when Moore produces his cases of ordinary things that we (therefore) can correctly say, we all feel at once how perfectly correct they are, and how absurd it is for any philosopher to condemn such a way of speaking. 'The philosophizing of most of the more important philosophers has consisted in their more or less subtly repudiating ordinary language. Moore's philosophizing has consisted mostly in his refuting the repudiators of ordinary language.'[1]

Now this interpretation of Moore's intentions

[1] Malcolm, loc. cit., p. 365.

certainly makes sense of much that he said, and attributes to him a species of argument that is, within certain definable limits, both salutary and entirely sound. But I do not think one can say that Moore actually had any such intentions. Most of the reason for this is that Moore was quite exceptionally careful always to say exactly what he meant; but what he actually said is not at all what he is thus represented as having meant. The fact is that he does not anywhere express the idea that ordinary language is *ipso facto* correct, nor does he argue against other philosophers for attempting, overtly or covertly, to alter it. He always presents the case quite differently. What he defends is always the *truth* of certain very common propositions, and not the propriety of the language in which they are expressed; and he takes the view that other philosophers have held doctrines incompatible with the *truth* of these propositions, not that they have merely rejected the common use of words. That much philosophy has consisted in 'more or less subtly repudiating ordinary language' is a *theory* about philosophical theories, to which Moore has at least never committed himself. He seems, on the contrary, always to have taken the more direct view that philosophers were seeking to arrive at the truth, can be supposed to have meant what they said, and hence to have seriously taken to be true what their words would naturally be taken to mean. He does indeed, in a sense, 'defend ordinary language'; but only, I think, in the sense that he regards it as adequate for our purposes, and considers that technical or other unusual ways of speaking are often more dangerous than beneficial. Much more important than this, in his own view, is surely the defence of the *truth* of common-sense *statements*—the insistence that (however difficult their analysis may be) no philosophical argument whatever could show them to be false, or even doubtful.

If, then, we cannot say that Moore himself believed that other philosophers were engaged in 'repudiating ordinary language', what did he consider that they were doing? How did he account for the extraordinary fact that, as he says, they frequently asserted doctrines incompatible with what they themselves knew to be true? Philosophy, one might think, must be a most peculiar subject, if this is what philosophers so often are led to; but what does the peculiarity consist in? I believe that Moore never had a general answer to this question. He certainly believed that philosophers were often confused and often argued invalidly, and thus were often led into making assertions that were unclear, or false, or unfounded. But to the question why in particular these assertions so often had the air of paradox, of running counter to our very simplest convictions, he seems to me to have had no answer to give. It is one of the chief merits of his work that it raises this question clearly and sharply; the unshakeable ordinariness of his own assertions makes us most keenly aware of the extreme oddness of the views he objected to; but he does not tell us what exact sort of oddness it is. He believes that his opponents have argued badly; but in that, by itself, there is nothing particularly odd. He would perhaps have suggested,

c

though this is not certain, that other philosophers had commonly failed to distinguish between debating the truth or falsehood of a proposition, and debating the question of its correct analysis. Perhaps sometimes, entangled in the quite genuine difficulties of analysing even some very simple proposition, they had been betrayed by defects of clarity into believing the truth of the proposition to be in question. But in fact he seems commonly to have rested in the straightforward belief that philosophers, through confusion or fallacy or both, were apt to say things that were quite clearly untrue; that whatever the reasons may have been for this odd state of affairs, it was essential first to insist that the plain truths they questioned or denied were true; and that then it was proper to raise, in a comparatively clear atmosphere, the question how these truths ought to be *analysed*.

What then was involved in this notion of analysis? The problem of giving an analysis of a proposition was thought to be, in a sense, just the problem of saying what the proposition *meant*. One might be inclined to object at once that, if so, the task of analysis ought not to be so very laborious as Moore both says, and by his practice often seems to show, that it is—for do we not all, by his own admission, already know the meanings of the sorts of propositions he considers? However, a first reply to this objection would be that, though certainly we all do know what is meant by, for instance, the proposition that this is a hand—though we all do understand the sentence 'This is a hand', as one who did not know English would not understand it—yet we may not be able, without careful thought, to *say* what it means. To know how to use a form of words correctly is one thing; to be able to say how we use it is quite another. Part of the difficulty, then, in giving correct analyses may consist in the difficulty simply of saying quite clearly what it is that some phrase or proposition, whose meaning is probably not in doubt, does actually mean.

But Moore found the problem of giving analyses to be difficult, at least in many cases, for reasons other than this. In fact he involved himself in some trivial embarrassments by laying down conditions that any successful analysis must satisfy, which unluckily are partly too stringent, and partly too vague, for any analysis on those conditions to turn out successfully. But these minor difficulties can be fairly easily eliminated. At least two serious ones remain.

In the first place, Moore took very seriously a suggestion that is implicit in his metaphorical name for his enterprise. The use of the word 'analysis' carries the suggestion that something complex, something constructed, is to be decomposed—that its component elements or parts are to be distinguished, and its mode of construction from these elements or parts made clear. Now there are certainly some cases in which it is natural enough to think of propositions in terms of this seductive metaphor. A cube, for example, can be thought of naturally enough as a geometrical complex of planes in three dimensions; the proposition 'This is a cube' seems likely, accordingly, to be susceptible of analysis in terms of these planes, their number, their shapes, their mutual relations. It is arguable, no doubt, how exactly the analysis should go; but one would naturally suppose that it must work out in some not impossibly complicated way. But now what of the proposition 'This is a hand'? Is the notion of *being a hand* absolutely simple, a notion so basic and element-ary as to be in principle incapable of any analysis? It hardly seems quite so simple as that. But if not, what elements are they into which it can be analysed? What entities are they that are simpler, more basic, than hands, of which hands could be said to be, in some strange sense, constructed or composed? Moore had no doubt that there were simpler entities of some sort, on which our knowledge of hands (and of other such things) was in some way based, and which were indeed what we always directly referred to in uttering such propositions as that this is a hand. But certainly these entities have no familiar name, nor are we (in spite of our apparently incessant direct acquaintance with them) ourselves familiar with any such entities. Moore employed for referring to them the technical term 'sense-data'. He then seemed to be faced with two serious difficulties—first, that of making quite clear the meaning and use of this invented expression; and second, that of seeing how by its employment such propositions as 'This is an ink-stand' ought to be analysed. We know, perhaps, how people are related to crowds or how plane squares are related to cubes; but how are sense-data related to ink-stands? What *are* sense-data? Moore seems to have believed that analysis of almost any of his commonsense truisms led at once

to questions about sense-data, and these questions he
found so extremely difficult that, in spite of constantly
repeated efforts, he never believed that he had finally
answered them. It was as if, in pursuit of these
analyses, he always found himself falling out of the
bottom of ordinary language, and never at ease with
the invented language which he thought was called for
in that predicament.

Secondly—though this is not a quite separate point
—Moore involved both himself and others in difficulties resulting from the unquestioned assumption that
any analysis must be of a standard pattern. It was
always to consist in providing a verbal paraphrase of
what was to be analysed, in the form of a longer, more
explicit, but strictly synonymous phrase or sentence.
A favourite and significantly simple example was the
analysis of 'x is a brother' into 'x is a male sibling'.
But the fact is that very many of our words and phrases
are not thus tightly related to any more explicit
synonyms, and can only be made to seem to be so by
artificial devices. It is also true, and not less important,
that this sort of analysis may sometimes leave out
exactly what is of most philosophical interest. Consider, for instance, Moore's struggles with the concept
of *goodness*. He believed this concept to be unanalysable
—rightly no doubt in his own terms, since the function
'x is good' is indeed not susceptible of more explicit
synonymous paraphrase. But instead of regarding this
point as being, what in fact it is, wholly uninteresting,
and transferring his attention accordingly to the quite
subtle and important ways in which, and purposes for

which, the word 'good' is used, Moore evidently concluded that there was nothing more to be said. Goodness was simply unanalysable; and because it shared
this quite uninteresting property with, for example,
yellowness, he was able to assume that goodness and
yellowness were somehow *alike*. 'Good' and 'yellow',
he thought, were both names of simple qualities. The
very great and important differences between the *uses*
of these two adjectives appear to have escaped his
notice altogether, in consequence of the fact that they
do not lie where he was predisposed to look for them;
that is, they cannot be made to emerge within the
pattern of an analysis conceived so rigidly as Moore
conceived it. The constricting effect of this rigid
conception could be shown in almost any number of
similar examples.

What can be said, then, of the general effect of
Moore's work? We have taken note already of the very
powerful impact of his good sense, simplicity, directness, and argumentative rigour upon the china-shop
of Idealism. For the rest I believe there is divergence
between his theory, so far as he has ever had one, and
his actual practice. In theory he seems never to have
abandoned the idea that the goal of philosophical
inquiry is to establish very general truths about the
world—even, perhaps, about Reality as a whole. He
believed no doubt that such truths, if any such were
established, would not be at all so strange and surprising as his predecessors had held, and even hoped, that
they would be; for he did not conceive of the possibility that 'the Common Sense view of the world'

might prove to be untrue. Still, in theory he did not conceive of philosophy quite differently from his metaphysical predecessors. His practice, however, consisting as it mostly did in the pursuit of analyses, naturally tended to give rise to the idea that the business of philosophy is clarification and not discovery; that its concern is with meaning, not with truth; that its subject-matter is our thought or language, rather than facts. In its influence the practice was far more important than the theory. It is curious that just the same is true of his contemporary Russell.

Chapter III

BERTRAND RUSSELL

FOR more now than fifty years Bertrand Russell has been so fertile in ideas, and so prolific of words, that there must be both great difficulty, and some injustice, in reducing his work to the measure of our present inquiry. He probably disliked Idealism more intensely than Moore did, partly perhaps because he was less blankly immune to its fascination. He has certainly proclaimed, both more explicitly and more often, more numerous alternatives to its procedures and objectives. We must select for attention the most conspicuous of these, and consider first what his relevant predispositions were.

In the first place, Russell had been as an undergraduate a mathematician, and he soon became also a logician of a highly professional sort, the master and to some extent the inventor of new and newly rigorous techniques. He seems very early to have felt, with justice, that by contrast with his own work and that of a few others in logic and the philosophy of mathematics, the writings of most contemporary philosophers were exceedingly loose, amateurish, and obscure. He was fond of saying that philosophy ought to be, as it had never yet been, 'scientific'—not only not less rigorous and exact, but more so, than mathematics and the physical sciences. It is perhaps not true to say that Bradley and the rest had made no attempt to come up to this austere standard; but it could scarcely be held that they had succeeded very well. Accordingly Russell felt a strong desire to bring into philosophy some sort of professionalism, some technique, which would enable the subject genuinely to bear comparison with such patronized, supposedly inferior disciplines as those of the scientist and the mathematician. His insistence upon this point—his propaganda almost—was certainly of very great value in retaining for, and in some degree restoring to, philosophy the charms of intellectual respectability.

Secondly, Russell was suspicious, again with justice, of the fact that most metaphysicians obtained, and some deliberately sought, satisfaction from the theories that they devised. This seemed to him, again, to be grossly 'unscientific'. It appeared that the results of philosophical inquiry were at least allowed, if not actually intended, to be influenced by the needs and wishes of the inquirer—that for instance McTaggart's 'cheerful' conclusions were esteemed in part at least for the comfort they offered, and not solely because they appeared on investigation to be true. Against this he set up the scientific ideal of an entirely neutral, disinterested inquiry, altogether unswayed by such irrelevant factors as a desire for consolation, by religious beliefs, or by moral convictions. The philosopher's aim, as he wrote in 1914, should be 'to give an account of the world of science and daily life'. In the pursuit of this aim he should employ the most rigorous methods of logic, and not be distracted in any way by his personal needs or wishes or extraneous beliefs. The

method to be followed should be that of *analysis*.
Bradley, with his extreme distaste for 'bare conjunction', his insistence that Reality must really be a
seamless, undifferentiated whole, had of course insisted that analysis involves falsification, that it
can only lead us to unintelligible fragments, and hence
is the very opposite of the route to truth. Russell
scarcely troubled to argue against this. Remarking
pointedly that many philosophers were 'less anxious
to understand the world of science and daily life than
to convict it of unreality in the interests of a supra-
sensible real world', he simply dissented from Bradley's
opinion and embarked upon his own ambitious analytic programme.

There are of course enormously many different
things that might be called 'giving an account' of the
world of science and daily life. The sort of account
which Russell intended to give was, as he explicitly
admitted, metaphysical. The question 'What is there
in the world, and what is it like?' was not to be given
any obvious answer, such as a haphazard, empirically
collected catalogue of things would provide. The
question was to be answered much more generally and
more fundamentally. The aim was to strip off the
surface complexities of the world, and so to arrive at
and isolate 'the last residue in analysis'; and what
is to be found at this point of no further reduction will
not be objects of any ordinary and familiar kind. Unlike Moore, Russell was willing and indeed markedly
eager to emphasize that his findings would be very
curious and surprising. He would never have dreamed

of defending Common Sense; he would almost have judged it a denial of philosophy to do so. 'The point of philosophy is to start with something so simple as not to seem worth stating, and to end with something so paradoxical that no one will believe it.'[1] Mathematics and science after all held plenty of surprises; surely it was proper that philosophy should hold some as well.

First, then, what is it that Russell proposes to analyse? The answer, a surprising one perhaps, is *facts*, not things. 'The things in the world have various properties, and stand in various relations to each other. That they have these properties and relations are *facts*, and the things and their qualities or relations are quite clearly in some sense or other components of the facts that they have those qualities or relations. The analysis of apparently complex *things* . . . can be reduced by various means, to the analysis of facts which are apparently about those things. Therefore it is with the analysis of *facts* that one's consideration of the problem of complexity must begin.'[2] Facts, since they have components, must be in some sense complex, and hence must be susceptible of analysis.

Facts are stated in propositions, and propositions in turn are complex; they are put together, made up of *words*. Some words, however, are simple. Consider the word 'red', for example. It seems quite obvious that our understanding of this word is not a complex

[1] *Logic and Knowledge*, p. 193.
[2] loc. cit., p. 192.

resultant of anything yet simpler; in this case understanding can only be achieved by acquaintance with
what it is that the word 'red' symbolizes, that is, a
particular shade of colour. The word 'red' is thus not
capable of analysis, and may be said to be a simple
symbol. It is, in particular, a simple *predicate*. Contrasted with simple symbols of this sort, there must be
simple symbols of another sort, namely *proper names*
—the words, that is, by which we can refer to the
particular things to which predicates are ascribed. The
simplest sort of proposition, then, will be one which
consists solely of a proper name and a simple predicate. This sort of proposition Russell calls 'atomic';
and the facts that such propositions state are atomic
facts.

Now it is easy to see that out of atomic propositions
we can construct more complex propositions. We can,
for example, simply join two or more atomic propositions together with the words 'and' or 'or'. What
we thus arrive at Russell calls a *molecular* proposition.
But there are, as he holds, no molecular *facts*. Consider, for example, the molecular proposition 'This is
red and that is brown'; what would make this true,
if it were true, would not be one molecular fact, but
rather the two atomic facts, that this is red, and that
that is brown. Molecular propositions are thus said to
be 'truth-functions' of atomic propositions. That is,
their truth or falsity is solely dependent upon the truth
or falsity of the atomic propositions of which they are
composed. Hence, though we need to have atomic
facts to determine the truth or falsity of atomic

propositions, we do not *also* require molecular facts.

So far, so good. But from this point on Russell found himself compelled to say things from which many of his followers sharply dissented, and which remained for some years as centres of controversy. In the first place, he held that there must be *general* facts, not only singular atomic facts. Consider the proposition 'All cats are black'. This cannot be said to be merely a conjunction of propositions, meaning 'This cat is black and that cat is black and. . . .', and so on until all cats have been enumerated; for even if all cats *could* be enumerated, it would still be necessary to say in the end that the cats thus enumerated were all the cats there were; and here the element of generality has reappeared. What makes 'All cats are black' true or false, therefore, cannot be a conjunction of singular facts, but must be an irreducibly general fact. Next, he held also that there must be *negative* facts, since the truth or falsity of negative propositions could not otherwise be satisfactorily accounted for. And lastly, he accepted a peculiar species of facts corresponding to such propositions as 'Jones believes that the world is flat', or 'Smith hopes that the sun will be shining tomorrow'. The trouble here is that, although these propositions look complex, they cannot be said to be molecular in the sense explained above. The truth of 'This is red and that is brown' obviously depends in part on the truth of 'That is brown'; but the truth of 'Jones believes that the world is flat' is entirely independent of the truth of 'The world is flat'. For whether this is true or false, Jones may believe it. Hence, it is at least not clear that this sort of proposition is a truth-function of atomic propositions; and hence Russell felt obliged to admit that atomic facts alone were insufficient to make clear in what the truth or falsity of such propositions consisted.

It is not necessary now to go into the attempts that were made to dispense with these additional species of facts. Wittgenstein, Ramsey, Wisdom, and Russell himself all made great efforts from time to time to eliminate them. But at present the important point to apprehend is that they all shared a single ambition— the ambition, that is, of establishing the thesis that there were in reality only atomic facts, and in language only atomic and molecular propositions. These 'atoms', linguistic or factual, were the final, or the nearest approach to the final, 'residue in analysis'. They laid bare the essential character of language and of the world.

What made this ambitious metaphysical thesis seem plausible? Two factors can be distinguished here. In the first place, it had a kind of consistency with what had been, before the incursion of German Idealism, the most constant and perhaps the most fertile enterprise in which British philosophers had been engaged since the time of Locke. It had long been regarded as at least an important part of the philosopher's task to analyse the gross and complex constituents of human experience into their simplest elements; and it had always been assumed that to do this was to achieve a closer grasp of the facts, to learn something of the true nature of reality. The motives behind this enterprise had been admittedly various. Berkeley, for example, was fundamentally concerned to establish a peculiar sort of ontology, to show that we need not and indeed could not suppose the existence of anything but 'spirits' and 'ideas'; he was metaphysically opposed to metaphysical materialism. Hume on the other hand had been more neutrally interested in working out a completely thorough-going empiricism—in effecting 'reductions' wherever possible to the basic data of sense-experience. These philosophers tended to speak of words and 'ideas', where Russell would speak rather of propositions and facts; they proceeded also, by comparison with Russell, in a loose, informal, untechnical manner. But there is no doubt that in adopting the general aim of arriving at the simple by analysis of the complex, Russell and his followers were continuing a tradition which had long been familiar and seemed unproblematic.

But secondly, Russell was influenced more immediately by recent developments in logic, for which he himself had been in large part responsible. In his and Whitehead's *Principia Mathematica*, which was in a sense the culmination of work substantially initiated by Frege, he had devised a notation in which, as they sought to establish, it was possible to state not only the whole of logic, but also the whole of mathematics. The claim as to mathematics can be here disregarded, though it was of course of extreme importance in itself. What is of immediate relevance is the form that this notation took. It was explicitly truth-functional. That is to say, even the most elaborate formulae stateable in it

NB

were constructed out of a few very simple forms, in such a way that the truth or falsehood of the formulae depended solely upon the truth or falsehood of these simple forms. Theoretically, as Russell often insisted, the complex formulae were all of them superfluous; they could all be construed as mere abbreviations of other expressions, often doubtless very lengthy, in which there would occur propositions only of the simplest form, and one or two logical words such as 'and', 'or', and 'not'—theoretically, only one such word was held to be necessary. Now Russell often spoke of this notation as constituting a 'logically perfect language',[1] or at least as being intended to do this. Of course, as set forth in his book it had no vocabulary; there, the pursuit of complete generality had required the use of variables only, not particular words; but it included, he thought, at least the *syntax* of a perfect language. How then was this framework of a perfect language related to the sort of language we commonly employ? Here Russell appears simply to have assumed that it *was* the language we commonly employ, as that would look if removable imperfections were removed; that is, that his notation embodied the *essence* of language, and that where languages differed or common language appeared to diverge, it was merely that this essential skeleton was concealed. It was for this reason that the enormous assumption was made that all propositions whatever which do not themselves state simple facts must be truth-functions of those which do. Something like this was manifestly true of the 'perfect' language,

X

---

[1] See, e.g., *Logic and Knowledge*, p. 198.

and hence it was *assumed* to be true, though covertly of course, of any language whatever.

It ought to be observed that these two factors—the trend of the old analytic tradition, and the influence of new developments in logic—did not point entirely to the same conclusion. If one were influenced mainly by logic, there would seem to be no particular reason, except a desire for tidiness, to try to establish that the necessary primitive, non-derived propositions were all of one and only one sort. If Russell felt that general propositions must be admitted as well as singular propositions, logic would furnish no very strong motive for objecting to that view. But if one were impelled by, for instance, a Hume-like desire to arrive at the basic elements of sense-experience, to establish, that is, a general empiricist thesis, one would then have a motive for wishing to maintain that the *only* non-derived propositions were those which recorded the occurrence of particular sense-data. The combination of these would lead, as it did lead, to the attempt to maintain that singular atomic facts were really the *only* facts, and that *all* propositions were either atomic or molecular.[1] This thesis appeared to have the double virtue of reviving pre-Idealistic empiricism, and of applying to philosophy the well-proved and dazzling procedures of logic.

It ought by now to be clear enough why Russell said of himself that he offered a 'metaphysic'. He was, in the first place, clearly propounding an ontological doctrine—telling us, that is, what 'ultimately', 'in the

[1] cp. Urmson, *Philosophical Analysis*, pp. 95-7.

final analysis', exists in the Universe. Furthermore,
this doctrine was obviously not an empirical one. It
was arrived at substantially as a deduction, from a
non-empirical analysis of language, to the nature of
that reality which language describes. But it was a
metaphysical theory of a peculiar, though not perhaps
a wholly new, variety. If one considers the theories of
Bradley and McTaggart, one soon comes to feel, as
Russell had felt with such deep disapproval, that an
important purpose the theories were to serve was that of
giving satisfaction to their propounders. The same is
fairly obviously true of Berkeley's. But it is not in any
obvious way true of Hume's; nor is it true of Russell's.
No doubt it may have yielded him intellectual satisfaction, but it neither had nor was intended to have any
emotional, or religious, or moral implications whatever.
For this reason it is rather difficult to feel towards it as
one would towards some more typical metaphysical
theory. However, when one is told that reality can be in
principle *completely* described in statements of the form
'This is red'—or even, on a more thoroughgoing view,
of the form 'This that'—it is clear enough that something very strange is being said or implied about
reality. There is no mistaking the metaphysical tone.

We must next observe a most curious fact—a fact
which forms a kind of paradoxical link between Russell
and his supposed antithesis, Bradley. It had sometimes
been objected against Bradley that his own theory was
suicidal. His insistence on the satisfactoriness only of
'the Whole', on the non-contradictory nature only of
the Absolute, seemed to imply 'the necessary falsity

of every stateable truth'—that the only really acceptable statement would be one which stated everything simultaneously, but which of course cannot possibly be made. But if so, the assertions of which his own books consist must fall under this universal condemnation; if true, they themselves cannot possibly be true. It was soon pointed out in a similar spirit that the doctrines of Logical Atomism, if they were true, could not be stated.

This was the very singular conclusion of Wittgenstein's *Tractatus Logico-Philosophicus,* a work of impressive subtlety and power which presents difficulties of interpretation not less than, and indeed very similar to, those sometimes presented by a sacred text. The argument was this. According to the purest doctrines of Logical Atomism, a proposition can be stated significantly *either* if there is, or could be, an atomic fact to which it corresponds, *or* if it is a truth-function, however complex, of propositions of that sort. But most of the propositions which Logical Atomists, including Wittgenstein himself, purported to assert were not of either of these kinds. For these propositions mostly did not *state* facts; they purported rather to say something *about* facts, in particular about the relations between facts and propositions. But according to the theory itself such propositions cannot be significant; they purport to say what cannot possibly be said. Thus, Wittgenstein was led to, and heroically drew, the conclusion that most of what he himself had said was senseless; in an odd way, to understand his own book was to see that this was so, and to realize that, although perhaps he had succeeded in *showing* something, he had not really *said* anything at all. This thesis, laid quite early like a sort of time-bomb in the basement of Logical Atomism, escaped notice, or was nervously disregarded, for a number of years; when it went off, its inventor and fortunately many others had already transferred themselves to other premises.

It ought to be said here that it would be a gross injustice to suppose that Russell's work has been of importance *only* in that he was the chief expositor of Logical Atomism. That aspect of his work has been singled out for attention on the ground that it was the most influential, and perhaps also the most characteristic, of its many sides and stages. But, quite apart from his eminence as a logician, Russell has also written on an immense range of philosophical topics, never without effect. Where so much is done, very much must inevitably be passed over; but it must not be forgotten.

Chapter IV

LOGICAL POSITIVISM

CONTEMPORARY with the middle and later stages of the work of Russell and Moore was the movement well known as Logical Positivism. The slightly political suggestion in the word 'movement' is not inappropriate since, for a time at any rate, the philosophers of this group had much of the deliberate cohesion of a political party, and even a definite programme, platform, or creed. Their work at one time attracted a very great deal of attention; at least its existence, and something of its general character, was known in much wider circles than ever took cognizance of the work of Moore, or even of Russell. Their main thesis at least appeared, both to their friends and their enemies, to be immediately intelligible; if stated polemically, as it very often was, it appeared to be of very great importance; and in this country it had the advantage of being presented with almost hypnotic clarity and force in A. J. Ayer's *Language, Truth, and Logic*.[1] All this publicity has been rather misleading. The name 'Logical Positivist', once put into general circulation, has shown an obstinate tendency to stay there, and to be repeatedly misapplied with ever-increasing inappropriateness. More seriously, it is probably true to say that, partly because of its notoriety, too much has been claimed for the movement itself, both for good

[1] Gollancz, 1936; second edition, 1946.

and for ill. The variety of metaphysical writing
against which it was most vehemently directed was
already languishing, if not quite dead, by the time that
the movement was well under way; and its undoubtedly
high standards of clarity and rigour were no longer
new; they had already been set, if not surpassed, by
Russell and Moore and their followers. The movement did probably make some salutary impression on
minds unshaken by the milder impact of Russell and
Moore. But to regard it as even mainly responsible
for the near extinction of old-style metaphysics is to
make, I believe, an error of history. That enemy was
almost dead when the battle began.

The main features of the so-called Vienna Circle,
from which Logical Positivism originated, were two:
on the one hand an extreme respect for science and
mathematics, and on the other an extreme distaste for
metaphysics. Its main aim, which it is important to
bear in mind, was thus to devise some clear criterion
by the use of which science and mathematics would be
proved acceptable, and metaphysics by contrast would
be condemned. The Logical Positivists were not, as
philosophers, concerned with the truth or falsehood of
scientific statements; for this they held, rightly, to be
the affair of the scientists. Their proper concern, as
philosophers, was held to be with *meaning*. Accordingly, the criterion they devised was to be a test of mean-
ingfulness or significance, a test which the sciences
would pass and metaphysics would not. This criterion
became known as the Verification Principle; and most
of the literature of Logical Positivism is concerned with

the formulation, always disputed, of this principle, and with the application of it in its various forms. Leaving aside the tangled disputes over its proper formulation, we can say roughly that what the principle laid down was this: that the meaning of any statement is shown by the way in which it could be verified— it being assumed that verification must always at least terminate in empirical observation, or sense-experience. A special exception was made in favour of such analytic formulae as those of mathematics, which do not require to be empirically verified. But the alleged statements of metaphysicians, theologians, or other such persons were held, in as much as they could not be empirically verified, to be condemned by the principle to mere non-significance.

This principle has a number of curious and interesting features. Perhaps the most curious is this—that it is easy, though misleading, to represent it as startlingly radical and (admirably or deplorably) destructive; and that it is also easy, though again misleading, to represent it as wholly innocuous and almost a triviality. Suppose first of all that we regard it as laying down a really *general* criterion of significance—that is, in such a way that anything at all which fails by this test is to be declared to be meaningless. It then appears at once that not only metaphysics, not only theology, but also every single moral and aesthetic judgement, any judgement of value of any sort, must be regarded as meaningless. For it seems clear that nothing that we say in any of these fields can be verified solely by empirical observation. If seen in this light—and indeed it was sometimes presented in this light—the Positivist thesis looks terrifyingly iconoclastic. It appears that not only a few venerable theorists, but almost all of us, are being charged with constantly uttering or writing down words which have, unrealized by us, no meaning at all. But suppose next that we regard the principle differently; suppose that we remind ourselves that it began 'The meaning of any *statement* is shown . . .'. We may then say that all that the principle really implies is that, if some utterance is not verifiable by empirical observation, then that utterance is not a statement. And surely in this there is no harm at all. All that it really requires us to do is to reserve the appellation 'statement' for those of our utterances which are empirically verifiable, and to call the others by other names; and to do this leaves everything substantially just as it was.

But both these attitudes are in some degree misleading. It is certainly true that the first, most startling interpretation is mainly the product of misunderstanding. For it at least ought to have been clear from the first that the Verification Principle could have no application at all to forms of words which in no way aspired to the condition of statements. It does not make sense to speak of the verification of commands, prayers, promises, expressions of intention, and so on; these accordingly do not *fail* to be verifiable; and to say of them that they cannot be verified is to make a somewhat trivial remark which in no way impugns their linguistic respectability, and of course in no way implies that they are meaningless. The *general* conclusion, then, that non-satisfaction of the verification principle at once implied the verdict 'meaningless' was always a foolish misunderstanding. However, the principle can hardly be regarded, in the manner of our second interpretation, as utterly innocuous. It is after all by no means arbitrary what we call a 'statement' and what we do not; it is not a mere matter of free linguistic choice. To say a prayer, we would all agree, is not to make a statement. But to utter a moral judgement is a good deal more like making a statement; and some might well feel that something would be lost in a view which flatly declared that a moral judgement could *not* be a statement. And more seriously, are there not some propositions, those found in religious creeds for example, which can *only* be statements, if they are anything at all? If there are, then it must in their case be a serious matter to be told that they must either be empirically verifiable or meaningless. Thus, even if we bear carefully in mind that the significance of statements alone is in question, the thesis of Logical Positivism can be seen to be no harmless truism. Those who were goaded, during the '20s and '30s, into the excited defence of religion or ethics or aesthetics were really quite right in regarding the verification principle as no laughing matter.

It was probably supposed at one time, though not for very long, that Logical Positivism represented the introduction, at last, into philosophy of principles at once clear, simple, and decisive. It was however not long before complications broke out again. There were, for instance, always some who maintained that

the status assigned to sense-experience was un-
warranted. It might well be admitted that, if a statement has any definite meaning or content, there must
be at any rate some *difference* between the situation in
which it would be true, and that, or those, in which it
would be false; also that, if so, it must be in principle
possible that we should find out which it is; and further,
that the process of finding this out must involve having
experiences, of some sort or other, the occurrence of
which would determine the question. But why, it
might be asked, should it be supposed that these
experiences must be *sense*-experiences? To make this
assumption at once entails that only the most ordinary
empirical statements will prove to be meaningful;
but why should this assumption be granted? Are there
not, or may there not be, experiences, and hence
meaningful statements, of sorts quite different from
those which the Positivists admitted? In the absence of
any satisfactory account of experiences of those
supposed other sorts, this objection remained perhaps
somewhat theoretical; but it was also difficult to
eliminate.

More serious, however, at least at the time, was the
fact that, even in the judgement of Positivists themselves, there arose grave internal difficulties in their
position. These all arose out of the problem of defining
exactly what was to be meant by 'verification'. It
seems, for example, reasonable to say that, so far as I
am concerned, verifying any statement must consist
in my having, now or in the future, experiences of the
appropriate sort. But from this two odd consequences

seem to follow. First, does it not follow, according to the verification principle, that any statement, even a statement which purports to refer to the past, must *really* mean (so far as I am concerned) something about my present or future experience? If verification can occur only now or in future, can I ever succeed in really *meaning* something about the past? Second, can it really be that any two people ever mean or understand the same thing? Verification for you must occur in your experience, and for me in mine. Hence, what any statement really means must apparently be systematically different for each person who does or might hear or read, speak or write it. How then do we succeed in communicating with each other? What I mean, others can necessarily not understand.

To deal with this difficulty drastic measures were adopted. An attempt was made by some to maintain that this queer 'linguistic solipsism', this apparently ineluctable privacy of meaning, did not matter—that the general intelligibility of language could be saved without denying it. Others adopted the more strenuous policy of asserting that individual reports of sense-experience, though they appeared to be subjective, to be about the private experiences of each reporter, must really be understood as referring in every case to publicly observable, physical events. Thus, the statement 'I feel hot', for example, can be said to mean the same to anyone at all as it does to me, at the expense of maintaining that, even for me, it really refers only to the condition of my body, and not, as it appears to do, to my private feelings. This bold but astonishingly unplausible doctrine was given the appropriate name of 'physicalism', and unfortunately confused, particularly by Neurath, with a quite different thesis about the 'unity of science'.

A still more extraordinary development was this. It is clear that the Logical Positivist thesis was, in origin, an extreme version of empiricism; significant discourse was to be exhibited as firmly tied down to verifiable empirical facts. But in the end this bed-rock itself melted away. For reasons similar to those already mentioned in discussion of Wittgenstein's *Tractatus*, it came to be held that the relation of language to fact could not be a topic of significant discourse. There could be (so-called) statements *of* fact, which were supposed to be the concern of, broadly, scientists; there could also be 'syntactical' statements about the inter-relations of linguistic expressions—these were the philosopher's proper concern. But statements purporting to specify the relation of a linguistic expression *to* fact would belong to neither of these aseptic classes, and hence must be disallowed. If so, the assertion that any statement is verified, that is, found to be true, would have to be understood as asserting a relation *not* between that statement and fact, but between the statement and *other statements*. Thus, we might say, the non-linguistic component simply drops out of the picture, and continued talk of empirical facts must be held to be at best misleading. The Positivists, who in general were nothing if not devoted to their principles, made the best for a time of this position of linguistic imprisonment; but their fellow-travellers and others could hardly resist the suspicion that all was not going as well as had been hoped.

The gradual accumulation of difficulties in maintaining the simple purity of the philosophical doctrine, combined with the physical dissolution of the group as a result of the war, brought about the virtual extinction of Logical Positivism as a coherent movement. Its once canalized energies ran, in some cases, into rather different channels, and in other cases, unfortunately, into the sand. Some general assessment of its achievement and character will be attempted in the chapter that follows.

Chapter V

FIRST RETROSPECT

BEFORE passing from the philosophy of yesterday to that of today we may try the effect of an even more rapid, more Olympian survey of the position now reached, and its relation to a lengthier history. Very general remarks may be helpful, and are not always untrue. It is no doubt perilous to make them. But that cannot be helped.

In the species of Idealism which appeared so suddenly and violently in this country in the later years of the nineteenth century there was, perhaps, nothing fundamentally new. The notion that the proper concern of the philosopher was with the question 'What is the ultimate nature of Reality?' was a notion at least as old as Plato, and arguably older. Moreover it had long been felt, more or less confusedly, that this was no ordinary empirical question; there had been a persistent and quite proper tendency, as more and more aspects and departments of life and the world were made the subjects of systematic empirical study, to distinguish these as not within the philosopher's province. The philosopher's method of inquiry was to consist in reasoning. He was to consider—not challenging, or at least not challenging on their own level, the factual findings of other investigators—how Reality, how things in general, ought to be viewed, in such a way as to satisfy the demands of reason. Of course, what reason demands is not immediately clear; and in fact past philosophers could be quite illuminatingly classified in terms of the startlingly divergent answers they gave, or very often assumed, to the question what these demands were. What determined these answers might be said to be their various senses of what was satisfactory, ideally intelligible. Some found their ideal in tight deductive systems; others, very differently, in the notion of physical mechanism. Others again preferred explanations in terms of purpose. And there were some, as Hume in certain moods but pre-eminently Kant, whose concern was with the question whether *any* view could be both tenable and rationally satisfying.

Absolute Idealism can be distinguished chiefly as being a system for extremists. The supposed satisfactoriness only of the undifferentiated Absolute entailed the consequence that, in order to satisfy reason's demands, the whole apparatus not only of our, but of any, system of thought and speech must be dismantled, and a view substituted which might be occasionally guessed at or glimpsed, but which certainly could never be embodied in sober statement. In natural but perhaps unholy alliance with this novel extremism of thought, there occurred a striking rise in the temperature of philosophical writing. With honourable exceptions, the Idealists brought into British philosophy a species of vivid, violent, and lofty imprecision which even in general literature had hitherto been rare. That this was so was by no means unimportant. It helped them to convey a vague general impression that they were concerned with far deeper questions, and concerned with them far more seriously and intently, than any of their predecessors had ever been. This impression has survived in some quarters to plague their successors. It was doubtless not dishonestly conveyed; but it is certainly mistaken. It is not an indication of blindness or bias to distinguish between the importance of what is said, and the emphasis or eccentricity in the manner of saying it. That distinction is often extremely important in philosophy.

From the point of view of this striking but short-lived philosophical extremism, Moore appears as a far more extraordinary figure than Russell. Certainly, Russell's world of indefinitely numerous, independent logical atoms is the metaphysical opposite of Bradley's Absolute. Certainly, the kind of logic which he thought of as exhibiting the pattern of linguistic perfection, and therefore the true picture of reality, was as far removed as possible from anything that Bradley would have felt to be satisfactory. His respect for mathematics and physics was un-Idealistic. But there is a sense, even so, in which he was playing the same game. He had his own strange notion of the rationally satis-factory, and in terms of it tried to 'give an account' of the world. What was new in this enterprise (and doubtless exceedingly important) was the detail of its execution; its general character was, on the contrary, wholly traditional. Moore, however, was a quite new kind of important philosopher. Though he did not deny the legitimacy of metaphysical ambitions, he was himself entirely without them. If (as he has said himself) his passion for argument had not been provoked into action by the strange doings of others, he might never have been a philosopher at all. For, in general, he did not feel it to be difficult at all to make out a world-view that would satisfy reason's demands. He found the view we all hold, the 'Common Sense view of the world', to be perfectly unsurprising, undistressing, quite certainly true. Perhaps he would have wished to adjust it a little here and there; and, being what he was, this might have occupied him for quite a long time. But this was not what he was really interested in doing. Quite certain of the truth of most things that we ordinarily believe, and profoundly sceptical of the possibility of deciding on the truth or falsehood of large metaphysical theories, he engaged with astonishing pertinacity in the clarification—which he conceived as meaning the *analysis* —of any propositions, philosophical or otherwise, that engaged his interest. Part of the great interest and importance of this for others consists, I would suggest, in the fact that this is something which anyone can do —to practise philosophy in the manner of Moore, it is not necessary to have (as most of us doubtless have not) nor to pretend to have (as some at least would be unwilling to do) large-scale metaphysical anxieties. It is necessary only to want to get things clear. And this aim can be pursued, as it was conspicuously by Moore, with an utter absence of pretension, an air of intellectual respectability, provided otherwise by Russell but by Idealism at least not always. There are no

E

doubt many who also take satisfaction in the absence
from Moore's manner of writing of any aspiration to
inappropriate literary virtues. Philosophy as he has
pursued it can be seen to be work.

What then are the bearings in this setting of Logical
Positivism? Here the situation is decidedly an odd one,
owing, as so often, to discordance between theory and
practice. In theory the Positivists had made a most
radical departure. For they held, as it had never been
held before, that philosophers as such could have no
concern at all with questions of fact. The logical
analysis of language was not regarded, as it had been
by Russell and Moore and in some degree by all earlier
philosophers, as *part* of the philosopher's business, but
as the whole of it; it was explicitly held that there was
nothing else for him to do. Positivists sometimes
maintained, in defensive mood, that they ought not to
be regarded as revolutionaries—for had not all philosophers from Plato onwards spent much of their time
on the niceties of linguistic analysis? Certainly they
had. But it had not hitherto been contended that
language alone formed the entire subject-matter of
philosophy. Those who maintained that this was
radically new were quite right, and those who denied
it were, perhaps, less than ingenuous.

However, I believe that to a really Olympian eye the
Positivists, again, would look less extraordinary than
Moore. For in fact they had, surely, their own meta-
physical beliefs. Even if their attachment to the
Verification Principle is not, as it quite plainly could
be, construed as itself expressing a metaphysical

conviction, their later doctrines of Physicalism and the 'unity of science' fairly clearly express a particular world-view, a particular ideal of rational acceptability. They were no more reluctant than, say, Bradley would have been to throw over the plain opinions of the plain man, if these could not be squared with the demands of their peculiar principles. No doubt such disagreements were, in their careful moments, represented as not factual, but as 'syntactical' or analytic; but this, even if it were true, would not be decisive; for even the most overtly metaphysical paradox is not quite *ordinarily* at odds with our common opinions.

Continuing our lofty retrospect over the recent past, we may well be struck next by the very curious fact that all the successors of the Idealist empire, however variously related to it by practice or theory, had among themselves a strong family resemblance. Their interests, their principles, and even their prejudices turned out in fact to be remarkably alike. First, they had all arrived by their different routes at the view that the day-to-day labours of the philosopher consisted overwhelmingly in the *analysis of language*. For Moore this was simply the route to clearer understanding, a preliminary perhaps to metaphysical theory, but in practice taking up almost all of his time and attention. For the Logical Atomists the analysis of language was regarded as itself the key to metaphysical truth. Their whole thesis was derived in part, as Russell avowed, from the study of logic conceived as the syntax of a 'perfect language'; and the so-called 'location', through the fog of our imperfect language, of the ultimate facts that we really refer to, was to be achieved by the logical analysis of propositions. The Positivists were also engaged in linguistic analysis, officially without metaphysical ambitions; theirs was supposed to be the two-sided task, on the one hand of exposing the muddles of metaphysicians, and on the other hand of humbly clarifying the vocabularies of the scientist and the mathematician. Thus, in spite of their very substantial divergences in aim and disagreements in doctrine, what each party actually did was very much the same.

But the resemblance in practice went also further than this. All parties were alike, not only in their concern with language, but also in their predominant concern with a particular part of it. They were interested almost exclusively in statements of fact. This is not, of course, in the least surprising. The Positivists wished to distinguish the truths of science from the alleged truths of metaphysics, and hence were concerned to draw a clear distinction between genuine statements of fact and mere impostors. The Atomists, bent on the location of atomic facts, had of course to take ordinary statements of fact as their point of departure. And Moore was mainly concerned with the analysis of what was, or at least might perhaps be, *true*, and hence he too made statements the topic of his inquiries.

More interesting, perhaps, is the further point that certain *prejudices* about statements were also common to all parties. This is shown in the commonly accepted

notion of 'analysis', and in the commonly held conviction that analysis of this type was entirely adequate
for philosophical purposes. The search for philosophical analyses always took the form of an attempt
to formulate a sort of linguistic equation. On the left
of the equation was to be the expression to be analysed,
and on the right another expression, usually longer
and more explicit, designed to be synonymous with or
equivalent to the first—equivalent in the sense of being
entailed by, entailing, and being logically independent
of the very same things. It seems not to have been
doubted that language did actually have the rather
simple and perfectly rigid articulation presupposed by
this faith in simple linguistic equations; nor does it
appear to have occasioned any discomfort that they
leave out of account all questions of non-verbal
context—questions, that is, about the characteristic
situations or circumstances in which, or purposes for
which, linguistic expressions are typically employed.
The practitioners of analysis operated in effect with a
startlingly simplified picture of what a language is—
the picture of a firmly and simply articulated system of
expressions employed, not indeed without reference to
fact, but in other respects in a total contextual vacuum,
for the one sole purpose of stating things truly or
falsely. The Logical Atomists can be said to have
adopted this picture quite deliberately as representing
the real state of affairs. For others it was implicit
only. But it was certainly present. For unless one
pictured language to oneself in this way, it would be
unreasonable to attach so much value to the standard

procedure of analysis. It would be too clear that
analyses of the standard pattern might often be un-
discoverable, or if discovered, then often so very
thinly informative as scarcely to merit the labour of
formulation.

Thus there was in philosophical circles, say twenty
years ago, a large measure of uniformity in practice,
overlying, and to a great extent concealing from view,
considerable diversity in aims and doctrines. It is not
surprising that the situation was often then, and has
often been since, misunderstood. It has been particularly tempting, I believe, for commentators outside the
professional ring to identify, first, what in fact was
common to all parties—pre-occupation with analysis of
language; next, to take note of the novel idea that
this was the sole proper business of philosophy—an
idea sponsored only by Logical Positivism; and finally,
confusing this singularity of doctrine with the general
uniformity of practice, to decide that all philosophers of
the day were Logical Positivists. This was in fact not
true at any time. I am inclined to think that it was not
even true that those philosophers who really were
Logical Positivists were the most revolutionary or
radical figures. By profession they were. But by
temperament, by practice, and by force of example, far
more *difference* was made, I believe, by the work of
Moore. He was not only among the first to oppose both
the manner and the matter of the Idealist 'tradition';
he was also far more profoundly *unlike* its practitioners.
By comparison the Logical Atomists and even the
Positivists have very much of the look of traditional

figures. Their work has a truly 'philosophical' air
which would not have been quite strange, though it
might well have seemed disagreeable, to their predecessors. Moore's work is in essence so simple, so direct,
so wholly unprejudiced and candid, as scarcely to seem
philosophical at all. It is just argument. That, perhaps,
is its peculiar virtue, and the secret of its power.

Chapter VI

WITTGENSTEIN

1. Language

THERE can be no serious doubt that the most powerful and pervasive influence upon the practice of philosophy in this country today has been that of Ludwig Wittgenstein. An account of his work and its effect presents peculiar difficulties; but an attempt to provide one, provisional no doubt and very imperfect, must be made.

The causes of difficulty at this point are various. In the first place, chronology becomes somewhat confusing. Wittgenstein's *Tractatus* was published in 1919. For a few years thereafter he lived near Vienna, being at that time in fairly close touch with, though never one of, the philosophers of the Vienna Circle; and he had been in England from 1912 to 1914, spending part of that period in Cambridge as a pupil of Russell's. He returned to Cambridge in 1929, and from about that date onwards his philosophical work began to take on a radically different character. However, for one reason or another, it was several years before anything much was generally known of these new developments. Not only did Wittgenstein publish nothing himself; he seems also to have been strongly opposed to any publication by those to whom his ideas were imparted. Several years passed before even articles bearing the new character were generally available, and even these were, to say the least, unauthorized by Wittgenstein himself. At the same time interest in his work was so strong in many quarters that reports of it did in fact achieve a considerable though half-clandestine currency. These could not be regarded, of course, as final or authoritative; but by 1953, when his *Philosophical Investigations*[1] were posthumously published, a good many philosophers had been for several years more or less familiar with the trend of his work. It is thus difficult or even impossible to say just when or how his influence, after 1929, began to operate. It was certainly widely diffused well before 1953, but the peculiar circumstances of its diffusion baffle exact historical description.

The description of his work itself is also peculiarly difficult. The *Philosophical Investigations* do not even look like most earlier or later philosophical writing, and almost certainly suffer far more damage from being put into a nut-shell. The book consists of a succession of brief, often loosely connected paragraphs; as Wittgenstein says, it travels 'over a wide field of thought criss-cross in every direction'; it is full of unanswered questions, unamplified hints, imaginary dialogues, images, metaphors, and epigrams. One may well wonder how this impassioned notebook is related to the orderly, decorous, argumentative treatises of other earlier and later philosophers. Does it really belong

[1] Blackwell, 1953. German text and English translation by G. E. M. Anscombe. The paragraphs are numbered, and in what follows are referred to by numbers alone.

to the same subject at all? The fact is, of course, that it
does; but it is not at all easy to relate what is found in
its pages to what goes on elsewhere. Wittgenstein, in
fact, would not much have wanted to do this. He was
comparatively uninterested in the doings of other
philosophers, whether of the past or of his own time.
For the most part it was with himself that he argued
most vehemently.

Fundamental to the change in his philosophical views
which occurred quite soon after his *Tractatus* was
published was a radically altered conception of
language. In order to see what this change was, we
must consider very briefly the position from which he
began. This was in fact closely related to Russell's
Logical Atomism; it could be called perhaps a more
consistent, more thorough, and therefore more
extreme working out of some of Russell's principles
and ideas. Wittgenstein in a sense took these ideas
more seriously; he saw more deeply into their consequences. We have already mentioned his startling
realization that, if what he himself had written was true,
then it must for the most part also be meaningless;
and we have seen that he did not shrink from avowing
this. He also paid more attention than Russell had
done to the ways in which language must be supposed
to be related to the world of which we wish to speak,
and to the character of the 'logical atoms' of
which, according to the doctrine, reality was composed. On both points his views were ruthlessly
peculiar.

Like Russell, he located the real link between

language and reality in the relation of atomic propositions to atomic facts. His general conception of this
relation is well suggested in his own comparison with
pictures. In a picture of an object or scene, there is a
kind of correspondence between the parts of or
elements in the picture, and the parts of or elements in
the object or scene But these elements must not only
be present; their structure, form, or arrangement must
be the same—according of course to some system of
projection, whether simple perspective or something
more elaborate. Now 'an atomic fact is a combination
of objects (entities, things). . . . The configuration of
objects forms the atomic fact.'[1] But the 'sentential
sign' is itself also a fact; it too is a combination of
elements, namely *words*. This sort of fact is therefore
capable of 'picturing' those other, non-verbal facts;
and it is thus that language can refer to the world, can
mean something other than itself. What were the
elements of these facts taken to be? On the side of
language they were said to be, in a queer sense, names,
simple demonstrative symbols; on the side of reality
they were objects, 'particulars'. But a particular cannot
be, as Russell had supposed, such a thing as a white dot
or a red patch. For that a particular is white or red is
merely a fact about it; it *itself* is merely what *can* be
white or red, and can be said (misleadingly perhaps)
to be really colourless.[2] And since an object is what
can enter into a 'configuration', it must not itself *be*
a configuration; it must be simple.

[1] *Tractatus*, 2.01, 2.0272.
[2] ibid. 2.032.

But not all propositions of any actual language are atomic propositions, pictures of atomic facts. So what are the propositions that we actually utter? Here, as we have seen, the thorough-going answer was ready to hand; they are truth-functional compounds of atomic propositions. Atomic propositions are, as it were, the nearly-undetectable bricks out of which our daily utterances are built; and the rules of construction, hard though it may be to see that this is so, are (more or less) the rules of combination laid down in *Principia Mathematica*. No doubt we often utter sets of words which are not thus constructed; sometimes we do this through sheer confusion, sometimes (as perhaps in expressing ethical judgements) we do it for more serious purposes; but in all such cases it has to be concluded that we do not really *say* anything—our words have no *meaning*, for meaning is derivable alone, in certain ways alone, from atomic propositions.

Now it was, of course, always clear that this account of language was not any sort of empirical description; it was not based on observation. If one were asked simply to observe a language and describe it, one's account would certainly be utterly unlike this. Indeed it was a point constantly stressed that language does *not* appear to fit with this account, that one's natural impressions of it are utterly different. What this account was intended to be was an exposition of the *essence* of language; an account of its concealed foundations; an excavation, so to speak, to its deepest level. The attempt was to bring into the light what language conceals—its own hidden workings, its essential bones that are normally unseen beneath the familiar surface. The account offered was thus in no way *seen* to be a true one; it was maintained only that, if we think about the essence of language and neglect its merely superficial features, we shall see that the foundations *must* be as thus described.

It appears that within the space of a few years after 1919 Wittgenstein came to believe that this queer, non-empirical account of language was not, as it claimed to be, the exposure of something deeply concealed, but on the contrary the foisting of an *invention* upon the facts. He came to reject in particular three of the implications or assumptions of his earlier views—first, that language is essentially used for *one* purpose, the stating of facts; second, that sentences essentially get their meanings in *one* way, namely through 'picturing'; and third, that any language essentially has, though it may be hard to see it, the clear and firm structure of the formulae in a logical calculus.

Suppose, he now says, that we make a serious attempt to 'command a clear view of the aim and functioning of words'. The first essential point is to observe how various in fact these are. 'Think of the tools in a toolbox; there is a hammer, pliers, a saw, a screwdriver, a rule, a glue-pot, glue, nails and screws.—The functions of words are as diverse as the functions of these objects.'[1] We may be tempted, especially when we are doing philosophy, to offer some *one* account of the way words function; but any such single account is, at best,

[1] 11.

quite useless—as useless as would be, for example, some *one* account of what tools are for. What would be gained by saying, for example, 'All tools serve to modify something'? This really tells us nothing at all about tools. It is not even much use to say that there are many kinds of tools; for how many 'kinds' are there? 'How many kinds of sentence are there? Say assertion, question, and command?—There are *countless* kinds: countless different kinds of use of what we call "symbols", "words", "sentences". And this multiplicity is not something fixed.'[1] Words are used in giving orders, describing things, expressing wishes; in play-acting, translating, telling stories; in asking, thanking, cursing, greeting, praying. . . . 'It is interesting to compare the multiplicity of the tools in language and of the ways they are used, the multiplicity of kinds of word and sentence, with what logicians have said about the structure of language. (Including the author of the *Tractatus Logico-Philosophicus*.)'[2]

Suppose now that someone were to object that all these differences in uses of words were merely surface phenomena, that there must be some *essential* use of language concealed beneath them—as indeed Wittgenstein himself once supposed that there was. We can then ask, why *must* there be one essential use? Is it supposed that, because they are all called 'uses of language', they must have something in common? If so, consider the case of *games*. 'What is common to them all?—Don't say: "There *must* be something

[1] 23.   [2] ibid.

common, or they would not be called 'games' "—
but *look and see* whether there is anything common at
all.—For if you look at them you will not see something that is common to *all*, but similarities, relation-
ships, and a whole series of them at that. To repeat:
don't think, but look!'[1] To suppose that something
must be the case, instead of looking to see whether it *is*
the case, is one of the many short roads to philosophical
entanglement.

In short, 'the more narrowly we examine actual
language, the sharper becomes the conflict between it
and our requirement.'[2] We are constantly struck by
more and more variety in the actual or possible uses of
words, and borne further and further away from the
idea that language ('as such' perhaps) has just one use.
In order to bring out the full scope of this variety,
Wittgenstein not only points out various uses in existing
language, but also imagines possible languages, simplified in such a way as to bring their multifold variety
clearly into view.

Consider next the related idea that words get their
meanings in some one way. Perhaps 'one thinks that
learning language consists in giving names to objects'.[3]
But there are enormously many words that could not be
thought to be names of anything. Besides, what is
'giving a name' to something? Perhaps pointing at it
and uttering the name. But of course, if this is to be
successful, the performance must be understood in
the proper way; there are always many different ways
in which it *could* be understood. If you point to

[1] 66.   [2] 107.   [3] 26.

something and say 'That is oval', I shall thereby learn what 'oval' means only if I already understand that you are referring to its shape. And how does this differ from referring to its colour, or to the object itself? 'How he "takes" the definition is seen in the use that he makes of the word defined'—and since there are very many different uses even of common nouns and adjectives, it is clear that learning by the supposedly single process of being 'given the name' must really be no less various. Even naming has to be understood in as many ways as there are uses of names. 'What is the relation between name and thing named?—Well, what *is* it?'[1]—we have to look at particular cases, and *find out* what is involved in coming to understand words, learning what they mean; and we shall find that very many quite different things are involved.

Consider next the *structure* of language. Is it the case that the propositions we ordinarily utter are complex, built up in accordance with precise rules of construction from exactly specifiable simpler elements? Is it true that there must be certain exact logical relations between the quite diverse things that we say? Well, why should one suppose that this *must* be true? 'F. P. Ramsey once emphasized in conversation with me that logic was a "normative science". I do not know exactly what he had in mind, but it was doubtless closely related to what only dawned on me later: namely, that in philosophy we often *compare* the use of words with games and calculi which have fixed rules, but cannot say that someone who is using language *must*

[1] 37.

be playing such a game.'[1] It is even dangerous to say that a language embodying fixed and clear rules would be an 'ideal' language. For 'the most that can be said is that we *construct* ideal languages'; these are not, as for instance Russell had implied, better or more 'perfect' than our ordinary language—'as if it took the logician to show people at last what a correct sentence looked like'. 'We misunderstand the role of the ideal in our language. . . . The idea now absorbs us, that the ideal *"must"* be found in reality. Meanwhile we do not as yet see *how* it occurs there, nor do we understand the nature of this "must". We think it must be in reality; for we think we already see it there.' Though the most obvious phenomena of language seem to conflict with this belief in a fixed, simple, and definite structure, 'the strict and clear rules of the logical structure of propositions appear to us as something in the background—hidden in the medium of the understanding'. But 'where does this idea come from? It is like a pair of glasses on our nose through which we see whatever we look at. It never occurs to us to take them off.'[2]

But suppose that we do take them off and look again at the facts. 'The more narrowly we examine actual language, the sharper becomes the conflict between it and our requirement. . . . We see that what we call "sentence" and "language" have not the formal unity that I imagined, but are families of structures more or less related to one another.' The idea of an underlying 'crystalline purity' was not a result of investigation; it was a *preconceived idea*. The 'perfect language' of

[1] 81.   [2] 100-3.

F

NB

Logical Atomism was not a discovery, something uncovered beneath the confusing wrappings of ordinary language—it was something invented, which gave to its inventors the illusion that they had found it, could somehow see it to be hiding *behind* what they well knew to be apparently so different. But were they right in supposing this difference to be only apparent? With our spectacles off, we can see no reason to think so.

So far, then, what Wittgenstein has to say amounts simply to this: that language *is not*—not even 'essentially' or in some covert way—as he himself and others had once represented it. There is no one pattern to be revealed, no single account to be offered, no small set of definite rules. On the contrary, the forms and uses of language are inexhaustibly flexible and various; a language is not like *a* game, but like a whole family of games, and the rules for, the purposes of, the ways of playing these games are themselves endlessly diverse. To this we must add one rather different point, to which Wittgenstein alludes only briefly and occasionally. We must, he says, resist the temptation to think of language as something unique, something isolated and quite on its own; we must not make it appear to ourselves as something *strange*. Using a language is not only *among* the most ordinary things that we do—'as much a part of our natural history as walking, eating, drinking, playing';[1] it is also in countless ways actually involved in many other things that we do, so that it without them is unintelligible, and they without it.

Q?

[1] 25.

'To imagine a language means to imagine a form of
life'[1]—so that often the explanation, or the understanding, of language must bring in what at first sight looks
wholly non-linguistic, something, simply, about what
people are, and want, and do.

2. Logical Atomism

But now, of course, we have something that needs
explanation. Suppose it to be agreed, as I imagine it
would be, that Wittgenstein's new way of looking at
language, even in the rough description that we have
just given, is reasonable, realistic, clear-sighted, illuminating; and that by comparison the *Tractatus* account,
however powerful and impressive in its way, does really
look like a myth, a theorist's fantasy. Suppose it to be
agreed also, as it manifestly should be, that Wittgenstein and Russell were not less, but far more, perceptive
and penetrating than most of us are. How then could it
possibly have come about that they accepted this
fantasy, with positive fervour, as if it were a fundamental truth?

It is remarkable that, in his *Investigations*, Wittgenstein did not deploy any set, systematic attack on his
own earlier views; he did not attempt to say just what
mistakes were made, what bad arguments used,
what distinctions missed. Now his refusal to proceed
in this way, though it might seem to add to his readers'
difficulties, was deliberate. For he believed that what
lay behind the old way of thinking was not a mistake of
fact or logic, nor even a cluster of such mistakes, but

[1] 19.

something better called a *superstition*. And how is one
to deal with a superstitious man? Suppose he believes
that natural events are the work of demons. It would
not help him to say, for example, 'But look, it is only the
match that makes the paper catch fire; it really isn't
true that there is a demon at work'—for until one has
somehow shaken or removed his entire system of
queer ideas, he can only see the phenomena you
show him in the light of them, still as the work of
demons. What we need is not to point out this mistake
or that, but 'to turn our whole examination round'.[1]
It is not, to put the point rather differently, that Russell
and Wittgenstein were not intelligent enough to
detect mistakes and flaws in their reasoning; it was as
if their intelligence was 'bewitched'; they did not
simply overlook the true facts of the case, but in some
way were *unable* to see those facts in the natural way.
We have, then, not to detect mistakes, but to dethrone
a superstition, defeat a bewitchment; it is the *source*
of the trouble that is to be exposed, not the errors which
were simply its natural manifestations.

What then was the source, or were the sources, of the
superstition? Here we find a curious position. The
source of the superstitious beliefs about language is, as
Wittgenstein argues, language itself. We have to
resist 'the bewitchment of our intelligence by means of
language', superstitions 'produced by grammatical
illusions', 'through a misinterpretation of our forms of
language';[2] therefore, we must look 'into the workings
of our language, and that in such a way as to make us

[1] 108.   [2] 109, 110.

recognize those workings: *in despite of* an urge to mis-understand them'. We must make it our aim to 'command a clear view', in spite of the fact that 'our forms of expression prevent us in all sorts of ways' from seeing clearly what lies before us.

What is meant by 'the bewitchment of our in-telligence by means of language'? Something like this: there are in our language certain forms of question, for example, which suggest—perhaps because most questions of that form would receive—a certain form of answer; or there are, in general, forms of expression which suggest—perhaps because they often have—a certain kind of interpretation. Yet, in some cases, it may be that the form of answer which a question suggests is not really appropriate to just that question; or that, more generally, a certain expression cannot rightly be interpreted in the kind of way that its form seems to require. But it may be extremely difficult, and particularly so in the practice of philosophy, to recognize such cases for what they are; we may be unable to resist the suggestion of our forms of language, and hence persist in the attempt to find answers to questions, or to interpret expressions, in ways that are quite inappropriate to the cases at issue. It is, one might say, as if the surface of our language were thickly covered with well-trodden paths, and we were constantly tempted to follow these paths even when they did not lead in the direction we were trying to go.

Consider, for example, what became in the hands of the Atomists of the question 'What is a name?' What came to mind first, it seems, was a certain simple

procedure of naming—the object is before us and we
give it its name, as Adam did with the animals. But
to be named in *this* way an object must both exist and
be present to the namer. But can I not say, of a ship
that has been blown up and of which the pieces are at
the bottom of the sea, 'The *Britannia* struck a mine
and sank'? And in saying this do I not use the name of
an object not present, which indeed no longer exists?
Russell's answer would have been that 'Britannia' is
not a real name; no doubt I can *describe* what is absent
or no longer exists, but I cannot (as Adam did with the
animals) *name* it; so 'Britannia' must really be a
description in disguise, and so indeed must be everything we commonly think of as a name. 'The whole
business of proper names', Russell said, 'is rather
curious'—so curious indeed that he came to the conclusion that 'the only words one does use as names in
the logical sense are words like "this" or "that" ',[1]
words certainly which it would never enter one's head,
in the ordinary way, to classify as names.

But what was it that led him into this curious view?
What indeed made Wittgenstein at one time inclined
to agree with him? In this case, as in others, 'a *picture*
held us captive'[2]—the simple picture of names as
assigned by Adam to the animals, as thus confined to
the case of what exists and is present before us. This
picture is, undoubtedly, a picture of naming—'and
we could not get outside it, for it lay in our language
and language seemed to repeat it to us inexorably'.
It is true that the actual uses of actual names are in

[1] *Logic and Knowledge*, p. 201.   [2] 115.

most cases nothing like that which the picture suggested. But two forces combined to push that fact into the background. First—and this was another case of 'grammatical illusion'—the fact that the question 'What is a name?' seemed difficult to answer was assumed to be due to the fact that the answer was somehow *hidden*—that the *real* nature of names was in some way concealed *behind* the plain facts as to actual uses of names, so that these actual uses should be kept out of the way, should be not looked *at* but rather seen *through*. Second, in the course of the philosophical discussion names were considered without a context, not in use, but as if taken out of use for more careful inspection. But words out of use are apt to get out of control. Thus 'naming appears as a *queer* connexion of a word with an object.—And you really get such a queer connexion when the philosopher tries to bring out *the* relation between name and thing by staring at an object in front of him and repeating a name or even the word "this" innumerable times. . . . And we can also say the word "this" *to* the object, as it were *address* the object as "this"—a queer use of this word, which doubtless only occurs in doing philosophy.'[1] Words thus inspected, repeated, thought about in abstraction from any actual use are liable to pose as having most peculiar uses which perhaps none actually has 'in the language-game which is its original home'. The harder one thinks in such a contextless vacuum, the more hopelessly 'bewitched' one is liable to become; 'one thinks that one is tracing the outline of the thing's

[1] 38.

nature over and over again, and one is merely tracing round the frame through which we look at it.'[1]

More generally: the Atomists had been ostensibly concerned with such questions as 'What is a language? How do sentences *mean* something? What is a name, and what sorts of things can be named?' The answers to these questions were not obvious; and here the first 'picture' began to operate. If the answers were not obvious, then obvious phenomena surely could not be relevant to the problem; the answer must surely be something quite different, something which the things we all see merely conceal. What then? And here countless other pictures, 'preconceived ideas', came into play—the picture of a calculus with clear and fixed rules, the picture of naming, the picture of dismantling something composite in order to discover its basic components, the picture indeed of a picture and what it portrays. All these and many others combined to produce the conviction that language *must* be, could *only* be, like this or like that—and at the same time to keep out of sight the actual facts, too obvious to be noticed or to seem important. All these pictures, so Wittgenstein suggests, are embodied in the forms of language itself. It is language itself which works to prevent the realization of its own character. To see how this is so is to have defeated the superstition. It is comparable rather with conversion than with the detection of error.

[1] 114.

3. Philosophical Problems

So far, we have sketched the way in which Wittgenstein came to see the problems of Logical Atomism. These problems he explained as due primarily to an attempt to impose upon language a 'preconceived', artificial view which was, when once one came to look at language with open eyes, startlingly inadequate to its actual variousness, complexity, flexibility; and the urge to make this attempt he attributed to an 'illusion', a superstition arising in some way out of language itself. From this point he came, even jumped, to the bold conclusion that *all* philosophical problems are of this type.

NB.

This conclusion was certainly not reached by induction. At no time, I believe, did Wittgenstein make any wide historical survey of philosophy in order to test his opinion against actual evidence. He believed no doubt that it was in fact true of his own problems, those with which he had himself been engaged in his earlier years. He perhaps thought also that his view *must* be true, if there were to be a distinct class of 'philosophical' problems at all. And perhaps he was also half-unconsciously inclined to make his view generally true by definition—that is, to classify a problem as philosophical only if it could be interpreted in the light of his views. Let us consider again, more generally, what those views were.

First, then, what is a philosophical problem like? Or what sort of problem is it to which we are inclined to give the name 'philosophical'? In Wittgenstein's

view what marks off such a problem is a characteristic
unclarity, a certain power to baffle and confuse. 'A
philosophical problem has the form: "I don't know my
way about".'[1] This sort of problem arises typically in
cases where certainly it is not ignorance that defeats us.
What is more thoroughly familiar to us, for example,
than perception, the use of our senses? Yet here there
has repeatedly arisen a most formidable cluster of
baffling problems. Conversely, if it *is* ignorance that
defeats us, we do not feel ourselves to be faced by a
philosophical problem. Questions about the structure
of the remoter galaxies, the causes of cancer, the
properties of the human nervous system, are questions
to which perhaps we do not know the answers; but we
see pretty well what sorts of questions they are, more
or less how their answers are to be looked for, and
whose specialized business it is to look for those
answers. Nor do we feel that a philosophical problem
arises where a question is clearly to be answered by
some sort of calculation—we see it as a question in
mathematics, for instance, or in logic, not in philosophy. A philosophical problem typically gives us the
impression that, although we know all that might be
relevant to it, yet we cannot see clearly; it is as if we
were lost and did not know which way to turn; or as if
we had become entangled and could not see how to
extricate ourselves. We see all the pieces of the puzzle,
but not how they fit together to form a picture. Very
often, this shows itself in the baffling fact that the
only answer to our question which seems to us possible

[1] 123.

is also an answer which we cannot believe to be true—
'But *this* isn't how it is!'—we say. 'Yet *this* is how it has
to be!'[1] It is not that we do not know what is the case,
but that we also seem to be driven to deny it.

In Wittgenstein's account of the ways in which such
typical predicaments arise two elements can be roughly
distinguished. There is, first of all, the plain but
extremely important fact that the verbal or grammatical
forms of our language are incomparably less various
than are the actual uses of words. Such grammatical
categories as *noun, adjective, verb*, are no doubt not
absolutely straightforward—no doubt one could think
of marginal cases that would present difficulties even of
grammatical classification; but still, it is clear in the
vast majority of cases how words should be grammatically classified, how sentences should be parsed; and the
complexity required for these purposes is not very
great. But the ways in which words are actually used
are enormously more diverse and complex than this.
'Pink', 'past', 'ambitious' are all adjectives; 'believe',
'walk', 'see', are all verbs; 'consciousness', 'table',
'cause' are all nouns. But cutting across these grammatical resemblances it is clear that there are immense
divergences of use. But it is not, of course, clear at a
glance what these divergences are; 'our grammar is
lacking in this sort of perspicuity';[2] and therefore it is
always possible that the very visible, grammatical
resemblance will lead us to think that there are other
resemblances, and even prevent us from noticing that
there are not.

[1] 112.   [2] 122.

It should not be supposed that this possible way of being misled is surely too simple and obvious to be a philosophical danger. It would be possible to illustrate its workings in many hundreds of actual cases. But let us take one to serve as a specimen. Moore, in examining the old Idealist contention that time is not real, was once led to raise the question, what the word 'real' means. But he considers this question in a very peculiar way. We apply the word 'real' to many things, to things of all kinds—we speak of a real (as opposed to an illusory) advantage, of a real (as opposed to a false) beard, of a real (as opposed to a toy) pistol, of real (as opposed to hallucinatory) pink rats; we employ the word, that is, to exclude a wide variety of oddities, defects, or deviations, it being as a rule quite clear from the context what exactly we mean to exclude in a particular case. Moore, however, raises his question in this way: what *property* is it that we mean to assert that all those things which we call 'real' have in common? Now there is, fairly clearly, no such property at all. When I say that the juvenile delinquent had a real pistol in his pocket, and that a long spell in a reformatory would be of real benefit to him, I do not in the least mean to assert that the benefit and his pistol have a property in common; but rather to make clear that the pistol was not a toy, and that the benefit would not be negligible. Why then did Moore assume, as the form of his question shows that he did, that there *must* be *one* property of 'reality'? Was it not because he thought of the *typical adjective* as being used to ascribe a property common to all those things to which it applies, and assumed that the word 'real' must be used in this way because it too is grammatically an adjective? That is, the very visible adjectival grammar of the word produced an 'illusion' as to its actual use. Moore in fact fell victim to a similar but more notorious illusion in his discussion of 'good' in *Principia Ethica*; this word too, he thought, must connote an 'indefinable' *quality*.

Rather different from but closely connected with this first point is our liability to be swayed, or even 'enslaved', by what Wittgenstein often calls 'pictures', or what could also be called *models* or *standard cases*. In a sense this point includes the first, since it may sometimes occur that a grammatical resemblance induces us to try to assimilate the use of a word to that of some other word of the same grammatical type, which we think of as exhibiting *the*, or the *standard*, use of words of that type. But the issues involved here may go far beyond grammar. Consider, as a simplified example, the notion of *proof*. Now there are proofs of many sorts—geometrical proofs, scientific proofs, police-court proofs, proofs of the pudding in the eating, and many others. But it may be that a philosopher becomes obsessed with *one* kind of proof, a particular 'picture' or model or standard of what it is to prove something; and so long as this picture retains its exclusive hold, he may feel obliged to maintain in the teeth of paradox that nothing else is really a proof at all, perhaps even that we do not really *know* anything but what can be proved in his ideal or standard way. Or it may be simply that he feels perplexed by proofs of any other sort—they may seem to him, however familiar, to be puzzling, because they do not fit in with his picture of a proof. There is, Wittgenstein thought, a characteristic way in which such puzzlement as this may arise and then become chronic: there is a certain temptation to suppose that such a question as 'What is a proof?' is a question to be answered just by *thinking*, as it were by inwardly surveying the idea of a proof—by attempting to discern, as Moore often put it, 'what comes before our minds', when we say 'a *proof*'. It is against this notion that Wittgenstein directs the injunction 'Don't think, but look!' For 'does the whole *use* of the word come before my mind, when I *understand* it in this way?'[1] No—the same picture, whatever it may be, simply presents itself over and over again; I repeatedly 'trace round the frame through which I look at it'; constantly seem to confirm my preconceived idea; and never think of *looking to see* what in fact proofs are, how many kinds of procedures are all called 'proofs', and how familiar really these various procedures are.

What then is the remedy for this predicament? The actual uses of the word must be identified and described. It is not, of course, that we do not know what the word in question means; no doubt we are well able to use it correctly. But we do not 'command a clear view' of its use. It is not that there is anything obscure or hidden to be discovered; what we need already 'lies open to view' in the actual uses we make of the word. So we need to describe these, in order to remind

[1] 139.

ourselves of them—'the work of the philosopher consists in assembling reminders for a particular purpose'.[1] And the purpose here is not only to make clear the use of the word, but also to oppose the powerful temptations that there may be to misrepresent it. It is true that there is nothing to be revealed, discovered, or explained—'we must do away with all *explanation*, and description alone must take its place.'[2] But this description must not be haphazard and undirected; it 'gets its light—i.e. its purpose—from the philosophical problems. These are, of course, not empirical problems; they are solved, rather, by looking into the workings of our language, and that in such a way as to make us recognize those workings: *in despite of* an urge to misunderstand them. The problems are solved, not by giving new information, but by arranging what we have always known. Philosophy is a battle against the bewitchment of our intelligence by means of language.'

4. Philosophical Paradox

Part of the explanation of the notoriety of the Logical Positivists lay, as was mentioned earlier, in their highly polemical and even abusive characterization of the efforts of very many other philosophers—in their zeal to attach the label 'meaningless' to many venerable doctrines, theses, and counter-theses. Now in a good many passages Wittgenstein says things which would quite naturally give the impression that he too took this view. It is worth inquiring how far he actually did so.

[1] 127.   [2] 109.

Certainly one does get the impression that, according to Wittgenstein, the philosopher's task today is to dispel confusion. 'What *we* do is to bring words back from their metaphysical to their everyday usage'[1]—and to do this, it seems, is to substitute sense for nonsense. Indeed he does actually say that 'the results of philosophy are the uncovering of one or another piece of plain nonsense';[2] this may seem purely and painfully destructive, but 'what we are destroying is nothing but houses of cards and we are clearing up the ground of language on which they stand'.[3] Again, 'when we do philosophy [i.e. when it is done in the old, unenlightened way], we are like savages, primitive people, who hear the expressions of civilized men, put a false interpretation on them, and then draw the queerest conclusions from it'.[4] He asks himself 'What is your aim in philosophy?'; and he answers 'To show the fly the way out of the fly-bottle'.[5] And where is he when he has made his escape? He is, it appears, exactly where he started; for philosophy 'leaves everything as it is'.[6]

I believe that, in fact, these and a few other passages tend to misrepresent Wittgenstein's real position. He did not really believe that philosophical doctrines were *plain* nonsense, *nothing but* houses of cards, that a philosopher was *merely* a fly in a fly-bottle. Why then did he say these things? They are, in the first place, here detached from their context—they do not stand in his book absolutely unqualified. Moreover they have, like so much of his writing, the character of aphorisms;

[1] 116.   [2] 119.   [3] 118.
[4] 194.   [5] 309.   [6] 124.

and the aphorist is not required to go to the stake for the literal truth of everything he says. It should also always be remembered that the philosophical 'illusions' which concerned Wittgenstein most deeply and constantly were those to which he had himself been at one time subject; and it is natural to repudiate one's own illusions with a vehemence and even rudeness that one would probably withhold from the illusions of others. When Wittgenstein thought of philosophy in the old style, he tended always to think first of philosophy in his old style; and certainly much of his more sweeping condemnation is primarily addressed to himself.

If for these reasons the remarks quoted above ought to be in some way discounted, how exactly ought they to be qualified or explained? In two ways, I think, both fairly obvious. In the first place, though Wittgenstein speaks of philosophical doctrines as 'houses of cards', he does not think of the business of constructing them as in any way silly or trivial. No doubt very many of the sayings of philosophers really are 'plain nonsense', no more and no less; no doubt they are sometimes the outcome of sheer confusion and nothing else. But these are merely the uninteresting cases. The interesting ones, although they too find expression in queer and distorted uses of language, 'have the character of *depth*. They are deep disquietudes; their roots are as deep in us as the forms of our language and their significance is as great as the importance of our language.'[1] If there is a prejudice which, arising from

[1] III.

some pervasive feature of our thought or language, from some 'picture' which our way of speaking imposes upon us, prevents us from recognizing the actual 'workings of our language', this 'is not a *stupid* prejudice'. Its source may lie so deep in our way of thinking that both it, and its removal, may be of the greatest importance to us; for of course the removal of a prejudice must be an affair of no less significance than was the prejudice itself. It may even be that some philosophical tangles are due to 'bumps that the understanding has got by running its head up against the limits of language'[1]—and this makes us at least see where those limits lie. It is true that the ordered description of the workings of language gets its importance only 'from the problems'; but the importance it thus gets is as great as that of the problems themselves. In the end they are simply removed, cleared away; but that they existed was never a *trivial* matter. They had after all the power to 'bewitch our intelligence'. Should treatment by psychoanalysis be regarded as trivial on the ground that it leaves a man nothing more exciting than sane?

The second point can be conveniently made with the help of some words of Wittgenstein's own. A philosophical problem, he said, has the form: 'I don't know my way about.' If so, then its successful treatment may indeed 'leave everything as it is', in the sense that it leaves me still in the same place. But it has not made no difference either; for now I *do* know my way about. The point that Wittgenstein had in mind was that it

[1] 119.

was not the business of philosophy to add to our
information, nor yet to alter our language; it makes no
difference of this sort. But it does make a difference in
that by it we may achieve a clear view, a grasp, a
command of what was indeed always there to be seen,
but had not before been seen in all its bearings and
connexions. We *leave* things as they are; but perhaps
for the first time we come to *see* them as they are.

Is it necessary here to add that Wittgenstein of
course does *not* suggest that philosophical problems are
all 'about language'? Of course they are not; they are
about knowledge, memory, truth, space and time,
perception, and innumerable other things. What he
suggests is that, though thus not *about* language, they
spring *from* language; they show themselves in distorted uses of language; they reveal confusion as to the
uses of language; they are to be solved (or removed)
by our coming to see and to employ our language
properly. It would make no difference of substance
here if one referred, instead of to 'language', to 'concepts'. This may sound more important; but the
problems were never thought to be *trivial*.

Even so, it would be urged by some even of those
who accept much of Wittgenstein's theory and practice
that the general impression which he gives of philosophy is excessively negative. This has sometimes been
urged, for instance, by Professor Wisdom.[1]

Suppose—to take an example which is, as short
examples must be, a caricature—that a philosopher

[1] See, for example, 'Philosophical Perplexity', in *Philosophy
and Psycho-analysis* (1953).

asserts that no empirical proposition can be known with certainty to be true. One might respond to this assertion in several ways. Moore for example, with justice, would have been much concerned with the fact that this assertion is obviously untrue. The proposition that, for instance, some cats are black is certainly an empirical proposition; and of course we all do know with certainty that it is true. So absurd indeed would it be to deny that this and thousands of other similar propositions are known with certainty to be true, that surely the philosopher who denies this must be saying something which he himself knows to be false. How curious it is, but apparently how common, that philosophers should behave in this singular way!

Now Wittgenstein, unlike Moore, would not have been surprised by the fact that the philosopher asserts what is obviously false; for he would have seen this as a characteristic symptom of a philosophical assertion, a signal that the assertor has 'lost his way' somewhere in the intricacies of language. His concern would have been directed to the question *why* the philosopher should make—should feel himself compelled to make— an assertion so extraordinary. For of course we do all know, as Moore maintains, that vast numbers of empirical propositions are certainly true. The philosopher cannot simply have failed to notice this; he must have been led into his assertion in spite of it; that is, he was bewitched. What is it then that has bewitched him? Let us suppose that he argued thus: If anything is to be known with certainty to be so, its contradictory must be known to be impossible; but all that we can know to be *impossible* is what we can prove to be self-contradictory; but the contradictory of an empirical proposition cannot be self-contradictory; therefore it cannot be known to be impossible; and therefore no empirical proposition can be known with certainty to be true. Now what does this argument do? In effect it identifies what can be *known* with what can be *proved*, and further identifies what can be proved with what can be formally *demonstrated*. It seems to embody, that is, a 'picture' of knowledge derived from the fields of mathematics or logic; and so obsessed has the philosopher apparently become with this picture that it has completely distorted his vision. It is as if it had driven him to *forget* how the words 'know' and 'certainty' actually work—to forget how many cases there actually are in which empirical propositions are, and rightly, said to be known with certainty to be true. Our task, then, must surely be to dispel his confusion by recalling his attention to the actual facts—by confronting his obsessive, exclusive picture of knowledge with all the facts that that picture does not allow for.

Of this sort of corrective procedure Wisdom has complained that it represents philosophical paradoxes 'too much . . . as merely symptoms of linguistic confusion'. It is not that the assertion is not both patently false, and also the product of linguistic confusion; it is both of these; but it may *also* be the product of 'linguistic penetration'. It may be that the philosopher who propounds a paradox of this sort has noticed something which is apt to be overlooked.

With our present example this might be worked out as follows: The interior angles of a plane triangle are equal to 180 degrees—we know with certainty that that is true. Some cats are black—we also know with certainty that that is true. So it seems that 'The interior angles of a triangle are equal to 180°' and 'Some cats are black' are in that respect alike. But some people used to think that they knew with certainty that the earth is flat; and they were mistaken. Now no doubt we *are* not mistaken when we say that some cats are black; but it at least makes sense to say that we *could* be mistaken, just as the flat-earth theorists *were* mistaken. On the other hand it makes *no* sense to say that we could be mistaken in supposing that a triangle's interior angles are equal to 180°; this *must* be true, in a sense in which we cannot say that it must be true that some cats are black. Thus, there is a respect in which 'Some cats are black' is much more like 'The earth is flat' than it is like 'The interior angles of a plane triangle are equal to 180°'; and in saying that no empirical proposition can be known with certainty to be true, the philosopher shows that he has been powerfully struck by this point, which it is easy to overlook. No doubt he expresses himself absurdly, even quite mistakenly; but he does so because he has really noticed something, and he makes us notice too. Such remarks, though false and confused, can be also 'illuminating . . . when they suggest or draw attention to a terminology which reveals likenesses and differences concealed by ordinary language'.[1]

[1] Wisdom, *Proceedings of the Aristotelian Society*, 1936-7, p. 76.

In short, Wisdom wishes to suggest that the sort of distortion which lies behind, and finds expression in, the assertion of a philosopher's paradox may be not only, as Wittgenstein would allow, interesting and important, but also in a sense *defensible*. The assertion itself, and the reasons given for making it, may lead us to notice something that otherwise we might have overlooked. No doubt this result could be achieved in a less odd and less misleading way; but there is something to be said, all the same, for the striking power of paradox. And does not Wittgenstein himself often speak in this fashion, paradoxically?

Chapter VII

CATEGORIES AND DILEMMAS

ONE of the more important events in post-war philosophy was the publication, in 1949, of Professor Ryle's *The Concept of Mind*. Though this book preceded by four years the publication of the *Philosophical Investigations*, its general aim is entirely in harmony with Wittgenstein's ideas. Wittgenstein said that philosophical 'problems are solved, not by giving new information, but by arranging what we have always known'. Ryle similarly writes in his first paragraph that 'the philosophical arguments which constitute this book are intended not to increase what we know about minds, but to rectify the logical geography of the knowledge which we already possess'. The importance of this book derives, mostly of course from the intrinsic interest of its thesis and arguments, but partly also from the fact that it was one of the first, is still perhaps the most large-scale, and hence has been one of the most widely influential, attacks in the new style upon an old family of problems. Nor is it rendered less philosophically valuable by the orderliness, clarity, and vivacity of its style, though these virtues have been thought to be dispensable, or even undesirable, by some who share broadly the same philosophical aims. Ryle has recently commended William James for restoring to philosophy 'that sense of the ridiculous which saves one from taking seriously everything that is said solemnly'.[1] His own book ensures that we shall not forget that, conversely, what is seriously meant need not be solemnly said.

What Ryle seeks mainly to establish is this. There is, he says, and has long been an 'official theory' about the mind, a very general doctrine or picture which has formed the background to almost all particular discussions in the philosophy of mind. It is Ryle's contention that this official theory, which he labels 'the dogma of the Ghost in the Machine', is not merely itself mistaken, but also has disseminated throughout this whole field a crop of interconnected and characteristic mistakes. There is need to 'rectify the logical geography' of mental concepts, not because in our ordinary transactions we find any difficulty in employing them, but because what theorists have said *about* these concepts and their employment has misguided them into a cluster of confusions; and the undetected cause of this misdirection has been the 'official theory', the unscrutinized 'dogma of the Ghost in the Machine'. In Wittgenstein's phrase, a picture has held them captive. Ryle's purpose is to break its hold, and to repair the damage it has done.

In describing the sorts of mistakes which he intends to correct Ryle makes use of a very old term which, some years before, he had himself put back into circulation[2]—namely, the term 'category'. A 'category-mistake', he says, consists in 'the presentation of facts

[1] *The Revolution in Philosophy*, Macmillan, 1956, p. 9.

[2] See *Proceedings of the Aristotelian Society*, 1937-8, pp. 189-206.

belonging to one category in the idioms appropriate to another', or in the allocation of 'concepts to logical types to which they do not belong'. The official theory of the mind, he holds, is both itself a category-mistake and a cause of countless category-mistakes elsewhere. His task is thus to correct a crop of mistakes of this sort, and to show that they derive from one, big, basic mistake which is of this sort also. Now this terminology is not, I think, wholly felicitous. It looks at first sight a good deal more precise and illuminating than it actually turns out to be, and thus has at least the deficiency of being liable to arouse expectations which are left unsatisfied. The difficulty is this, in the plainest terms: to say that some theorist has allocated some fact or concept 'to the wrong category' naturally prompts the two questions, first, to what category he has wrongly assigned it, and second, to what category it should properly be assigned. Both these natural questions presuppose, of course, that there are known and nameable categories. But in fact Ryle himself denies that this is so, and even condemns the idea that it is so with the strong word 'superstition'. He thus uses the expressions 'same category' and 'different category' without being at all prepared to say what category or which two categories are in question, and thus, I think, can be said to be refusing to gratify expectations naturally aroused by his own terminology. If one is not prepared, and indeed is deliberately unwilling, to say just what a category is, and what categories there are, can one really be entitled to employ the term 'category'? It is true that Ryle himself does not take this term wholly seriously. He has recently recommended it 'not for the usual reason, namely that there exists an exact, professional way of using it, in which, like a skeleton key, it will turn all our locks for us; but rather for the unusual reason that there is an inexact, amateurish way of using it in which, like a coal-hammer, it will make a satisfactory knocking noise on doors which we want opened to us'.[1] This remark, certainly, almost disarms criticism. Even so, it is not, I believe, unreasonably over-scrupulous to be ill at ease with the use of an idiom which has none at all of the precise backing which it naturally implies.

In any case it can be dispensed with. To allocate a concept to the 'wrong category' is, in actual practice, to misrepresent the use of, or to misuse, or both, the expression or expressions in the use of which that concept is applied. And this sort of misuse shows itself in two ways—in misrepresentation, first, of the ways in which expressions are related to one another, and second, of the ways in which assertions containing those expressions are validated, verified, or confirmed. Professor Ryle's contention is, then, in these terms that what he calls the 'official theory' of the mind both embodies and generates misuse, and misrepresentation of the use, of the expressions in which we speak about the mind; that these distortions generate theoretical problems and difficulties; and that *these* problems— not necessarily *all* problems—can be eliminated by the achieving of a 'clear view' of our use of this large and important department of our language.

[1] *Dilemmas*, p. 9.

In essence the 'official theory' as Ryle presents it hinges upon a radical bifurcation between mind and body; between physical things, events, states, and processes and mental things, events, states, and processes; between the 'external' world public to all observers, and the 'inner' life lived privately by each; between the mind, which for each of us is its own private place, and the body, which is publicly located in physical space. The important apparent implications of this picture are two; first, it suggests that, whereas each of us is well and perhaps perfectly aware of the events that make up his own inner life, he is only deviously and perhaps not at all able to tell what goes on in the inner life of others; and second, it suggests that statements 'about the mind' differ only, but also wholly, in *subject-matter* from statements about the body—that there are physical states and mental states, bodily acts and mental acts, logically analogous, but logically independent, differing only in 'status'. These implications have raised two insoluble-seeming questions—What is the relation between the mind and the body? How can we ever know what is in another's mind?—and have produced a host of particular misconstructions of those expressions with which we refer to and talk about people's minds. They have tended everywhere to impose the idea that, if some assertion is 'about the mind', then it has simply nothing to do with the body, and vice versa; and this in turn leads to the idea that, since the bodies of others are alone observable by me, their minds must be completely inaccessible and hence unknowable. As Ryle observes, 'absolute solitude is on this showing the ineluctable destiny of the soul'.[1]

In his book Ryle predicts that his attempt to annihilate this doctrine will be misunderstood in certain ways. 'I shall probably be taken,' he says, 'to be denying well-known facts about the mental life of human beings, and my plea that I aim at doing nothing more than rectify the logic of mental-conduct concepts will probably be disallowed as mere subterfuge';[2] again, he anticipates that he will be called a behaviourist. Both these charges, if charges they are, have in fact been made. But this is not, I think, due *wholly* to misunderstanding. For there could be said to remain in Ryle's book a residue, intermittently visible, of what are perhaps earlier thoughts of his own on this subject, by which these charges might well be supported. It is worth investigating how this is so.

The best general description—too general, certainly, to be very good—of Ryle's serious intentions might run as follows. He considers in turn a very large number and variety of assertions all roughly classifiable as 'about the mind'. The official theory of mind-body bifurcation tended to represent these assertions as, in the first place, logically quite unconnected with facts about the body and bodily behaviour; and, in the second place, as usually referring, when in the present tense, to presently-occurring processes or events, or presently-subsisting states, in or of its supposed 'inner' theatre, the mind. Against this Ryle persistently seeks to establish, first, that facts about the body and

[1] *The Concept of Mind*, p. 15.   [2] op. cit., p. 16.

bodily behaviour are nearly always relevant, and very often crucially relevant, to the truth or falsehood of assertions 'about the mind'; and second, that these assertions, even when in the present tense, are very often made true or false not by anything private that is *presently* occurring or is *now* the case, but by what publicly has been or will be, might have been or may be occurring, or the case. For example, that Jones is intelligent is presumably an assertion about his mind; but certainly his overt, publicly observable performances are not irrelevant to its truth; and what assures us that it is true or false is not something that we could (or perhaps could not) find *now* to be the case, by inspecting his mind, but is on the contrary our knowledge of his past performances and our estimate of his possible performances in future. This will serve, I think, as a painfully bald outline and example of the general respects in which Ryle seeks, in case after case, to show that the actual facts are at variance with the implications of the 'official theory'; and clearly he is not thereby committed to denying any well-known facts, or to upholding any such controversial thesis as behaviourism.

However, there are here and there in Ryle's book some traces of a more extreme, and in a way much simpler thesis. This is the thesis that there *really exist* only bodies and other physical objects, that there *really occur* only physical events or processes, and that *all* statements ostensibly referring to minds are really categorical statements about current bodily behaviour, or more commonly hypothetical statements about

predicted bodily behaviour; that, hence, there is really
no such thing as a private, inner life at all, and that in
principle everything about every individual could
be known by sufficiently protracted observation of his
bodily doings. It is true that even this extreme
thesis might be presented as factually neutral, as
merely an 'analysis' of statements about the mind.
But in fact it would be felt, and rightly, that its real
character was purely behaviouristic, and that by it
many well-known facts must be simply rejected. It
cannot, I believe, be wholly an accident that many
people have believed that Ryle's book presents this
thesis. It is certainly true that he frequently disclaims
it, and very much of his detailed argument is quite
free from any basis so narrow and restrictive as this.
But at least this simple and over-simplifying thesis is
not altogether absent from his pages. Could it be
said, perhaps, to be the Ghost in *The Concept of Mind*?
It is not, of course, difficult to recognize what it is the
ghost *of*; it is the ghost of the old programme of
'analysis', the attempt to reduce to some single
approved grade of basic facts such propositions as
seem to mention facts of other sorts. This kind of
analysis, resting as it does upon a very definite dogmatic
basis, is extremely unlike that species of unprejudiced
investigation the sole aim of which is to achieve a clear
grasp of the concepts we employ. But it seems likely
that Ryle, while consciously pursuing an investigation
of this latter sort, was nevertheless occasionally
haunted by spectral voices from what was, after all,
the very recent philosophical past.

There is another point at which Ryle's book has been criticized, but in this case, I think, quite unfairly. Ryle says that the 'official theory', the dogma, the myth of the mental ghost enclosed in the bodily machine 'hails chiefly from Descartes', though a rough genealogy might be traced further back through many theorists as far at least as Plato. Against this it has been objected,[1] in effect, that this myth or picture 'lies in our language', to use Wittgenstein's phrase—that very many of our ordinary ways of speaking and thinking, and ways of speaking also in languages other than ours, already strongly imply some such view without help or hindrance from any philosophers. This is true, no doubt; but Ryle does not deny it. What he objects to is the explicitly formulated *theory* erected on this basis, the theoretical mistakes which plain men, naturally enough, do not commonly make, but which many unwary theorists have made. It might be denied, what Ryle does not unqualifiedly assert, that the 'official theory' was devised mainly by Descartes; but it is surely absurd to maintain that it was not devised by any theorist at all. For theories do not formulate themselves without human aid. To find in our language many idioms suggestive of such a theory certainly entitles one to maintain that the theorists' doctrine was not arbitrary, foolish, and inexcusable. But Ryle does not suggest that it was; he claims only that it has been grossly misleading; and so, certainly, it has.

In 1954 Ryle published a little book in which he

[1] See, for example, S. Hampshire, *Mind*, April 1950, p. 239.

dealt with a number of separate but similar problems under the general title *Dilemmas*. The bond between the problems there discussed is a certain similarity in the ways they arise, a common feature which also accounts for their appearing as *philosophical* problems. The common feature is this. It is quite often the case that a certain kind of subject-matter, a certain field of facts or events or, in general, phenomena, can be the topic of more than one kind of inquiry, or theory, or science, or way of thinking. If so, it may happen that the conclusions or opinions on that topic arrived at in one way may seem to be in irreconcilable conflict with those arrived at in another way. We may believe, and indeed may have the best of reasons to believe, that each way of thinking is perfectly proper, and that the conclusions arrived at by each route are thoroughly well-founded; yet we still may feel ourselves obliged to think that one conclusion or set of conclusions must invalidate its rival. It is clear that this sort of intellectual *impasse* does not present us with an ordinary, departmental difficulty such as may arise *within* any theory or science or way of thinking; it is located rather on the boundaries of, or in the area between, one way of thinking and another. Its resolution, therefore, cannot be the special task of any *one* of the competing modes or systems of thought. It is in fact a task of the disentangling, straightening-out variety which is the characteristic business of philosophy.

'Dilemmas' of this general sort may differ considerably among themselves. They may be sometimes no more than puzzles, though doubtless perplexing enough

H

as such. There is, for example, the argument of Zeno
which appears to prove that Achilles in his race with the
tortoise can never catch up with, let alone overtake,
the tortoise which admittedly moves more slowly than
he does. This conflicts with our conviction that faster
runners can overhaul slower ones. But in this sort of
case we do not really hesitate between the dilemma's
horns. We know perfectly well that our ordinary
conviction is correct, so that the problem is merely
that of exposing the illusion that must lurk somewhere
in the contrary argument. But other cases are by no
means so clear-cut as this. Professor Ryle points out,
though he does not much discuss, the fact that there
has sometimes been thought to be a conflict between
religious or theological doctrines, and scientific
theories or discoveries. In such a case as this, there
would not be any general or immediate agreement that
one party or the other was certainly in the right; it is
not a matter merely of detecting the trick by which
something we all know to be true is seemingly disproved. It is not even clear whether the apparent
conflict is merely apparent, or genuine. It may be the
case that the dilemma is really illusory, that when
confusions are cleared away it can be seen that the
apparent antagonists are not really opposed; but it
may also turn out that the conflict is a genuine one,
requiring that one party must yield some ground to the
other. If so, the further question arises, which party
must retire. Even more complex is a case of very
venerable antiquity which is, however, still full of life
—the case of the apparent incompatibility between the

reliance we all place on the use of our senses, and scientific accounts of the processes or mechanism of sense-perception. The findings of, in particular, the neuro-physiologist have often been thought to entail that our senses cannot possibly inform us directly of the character of our environment in the way that we commonly suppose that they do, perhaps even that they cannot yield us any such information at all. It has certainly, and no doubt properly, not been thought obvious that the appearance of conflict in this case must be an illusion. Many scientists, and some philosophers, have taken it to be genuine, concluding usually, but not always, that our common convictions ought to be revised. But here there is the further complication that the horns of the dilemma are in any case not independent of one another; the evidence on which the scientific theory is founded is acquired by just that use of the ordinary senses which in the end the theory appears to condemn as unreliable. So what are we to say? Does it follow that the theory must be rejected as inconsistent, since it assumes to be true what it also purports to disprove? Or must reliance on the senses be condemned, for the reason that to rely on them leads to the conclusion that they cannot be trusted? There are here dilemmas within a dilemma. And here Ryle says, echoing Wittgenstein's remark that his aim was 'to show the fly the way out of the fly-bottle', that 'I buzz but I do not get clear'.[1]

Long before he had come to speak in terms of categories or of dilemmas, Ryle had begun to see the

[1] *Dilemmas*, p. 92.

tasks of philosophy very much in the way that he was later to describe in those idioms. In 1931 he had put forward the idea that 'philosophical analysis' might be 'the sole and whole function of philosophy', and that its aim was 'the detection of the sources in linguistic idioms of recurrent misconstructions and absurd theories'.[1] This, at that time, was advanced thinking indeed.

[1] *Systematically Misleading Expressions.* See *Logic and Language,* First Series, ed. Flew.

Chapter VIII

A QUALIFICATION

At this point one ought, I believe, to be beginning to feel that Wittgenstein's (and Ryle's) account of philosophical problems requires, in a certain respect, to be reconsidered. Wittgenstein at least appears to have intended his general remarks about philosophical problems to apply to *all* such problems; his words at any rate convey the impression that a certain generality and exhaustiveness are claimed. This perhaps ought not to be taken too seriously. He was, as we have said, not greatly interested in the history of philosophy, and probably would not have wished deliberately to assert that what every philosopher, historically accepted as such, had actually done was what he described 'philosophers' as doing. Nevertheless, the impression of exhaustiveness should not be allowed to stand, if one believes that it would be substantially mistaken.

My aim at present is a limited one. In a later chapter I shall have to describe certain kinds of inquiry which by any reasonable test should be accepted as philosophical, but which are very different indeed from any that Wittgenstein envisaged. At the moment I wish only to do something less than this. I wish to raise the question whether philosophical problems, which certainly *are* of the sort that he had in view, do all *arise* in the way that he suggested. Let us, that is, suppose for the moment at least that in every case 'the results of philosophy are the uncovering of one or another piece of plain nonsense'—that some philosophers lose their way, become bewitched and bemused, and in consequence profess paradoxical or extraordinary opinions, while other (or with luck even the same) philosophers seek, by the production of well-chosen and well-deployed 'reminders', to defeat the enchantment and re-establish good sense. We now have to ask how this situation arises—why it is that certain theorists should thus lose their way, and give occasion to themselves or others for remedial treatment.

We have already seen something of Wittgenstein's own answer to this question: 'Philosophy is a battle against the bewitchment of our intelligence *by means of language*', against false notions 'produced by *grammatical illusions*'. But now we must consider more carefully what exactly this answer amounts to. What is meant by the expression 'by means of language'? At an earlier stage we mentioned, but did not take much care to distinguish, two rather different interpretations. There is, first, the important point that 'grammar'—the more obvious, more literally 'formal' differences between words and expressions—is much less complex than, and hence does not reliably reflect, the many differences in actual use of words and expressions. 'Our grammar is lacking in this sort of perspicuity.' Hence, *particularly* in philosophy— particularly, that is, when words and expressions or the 'concepts' they represent are being, not actually used, but only thought about—there is a constant temptation to misrepresent actual uses. This may take the form of oversimplification, a failure to observe the full range or variety of uses; it may take the form, alternatively or additionally, of mistaken assimilation —of an attempt to treat some expression as resembling another in use, which in fact it resembles only grammatically. It is, I think, unquestionable that many problems have arisen and do arise in this sort of way; and I also think that one might very well describe such problems as being conjured into existence 'by means of language'. For they do not only consist, or perhaps reveal themselves, in distortions and misuses of language—that they arise at all is attributable to a feature of language itself, to the disparity, that is, between 'grammar' or linguistic 'form', and the far more complex and various uses of words and expressions. Our concepts, one might say, are more complex than our linguistic forms; our language often conceals differences, and may sometimes falsely suggest resemblances, between the concepts that we employ; and hence, though in practice we fairly seldom misuse those concepts, in philosophy we are inveterately liable to misdescribe their uses, and so to fall into conceptual entanglement.

Second, there is the matter of the power to confuse of what Wittgenstein calls 'pictures', preconceived ideas, Procrustean beds into which we may attempt with more or less intellectual discomfort to force phenomena that are really not of the right shapes and sizes. Now it might perhaps be suggested that the matter here at issue is really the same as that which we have just considered. Does not Wittgenstein say that

such pictures 'lie in our language'? Does not one who
attempts to assimilate 'good', say, to 'yellow' reveal
himself as being under the spell of an oversimplified,
preconceived 'picture' of the function of adjectives,
and is not this sort of misguided assimilation precisely
such as we have already admitted to be brought on
'by means of language'? Yes—but I think it is easy to
see that pictures which, in this sense, 'lie in our
language' are a special case of something more general.
It is true that, in these particular cases, the formation
of the picture or preconceived idea could plausibly be
attributed to the features of language—in general, to
our 'grammar''s want of the appropriate sort of
'perspicuity'; but this is only *one* way in which a
theorist may come to be damagingly saddled with a
preconceived idea. There are, unfortunately, a great
many others; and in most of these others it seems to me
not at all appropriate to speak of the bewitchment as
being worked 'by means of language'.

Let us consider an example, which might seem at first
sight very conformable with Wittgenstein's view, but
which in fact illustrates a large class of exceptions to it.
Russell at one time propounded the typically philosophical paradox that, when for example a physiologist
examines the brain of an animal, 'what the physiologist
sees is in his own brain'[1]—that although one might
commonly suppose that what he sees is in, or indeed
is, the brain of the animal, this cannot be and is not
in fact the case. One can see no doubt, even without
any help from Moore, that something here has gone

[1] *An Outline of Philosophy*, 1927, p. 140.

seriously wrong. Russell's dictum is hardly even paradoxical; it is simply untrue. Except in the unlikely event that the top of his skull had been removed without loss of consciousness and suitable mirrors adjusted, neither a physiologist nor anyone else would *ever* see anything in his own brain. What can have led Russell into conflict with this very obvious fact?

Russell's argument runs simply enough. Perception, he rightly observes, is causally dependent upon conditions and events in the physical world. In the ordinary case in which, as I should ordinarily say, I see some object, there occurs a continuous chain of events in that object, in intervening space, in my eye, my nervous system, and my brain. Now at some point in my brain this chain of events either comes to an end, or, more probably, reverses its direction—there is set up an outgoing chain which may terminate in my making some overt 'response' to the object. At the point at which this change of direction occurs—somewhere, that is, in my own brain—is located what Russell calls a 'percept'. But this, he holds, is what I really see. For it is this that is at the inside end—*my* end—of the whole elaborate chain of events; the object itself is at the other end, is the indirect and comparatively remote *cause* of my percept. Thus the percept, which I really see, is in my own brain; and the object, which I naïvely suppose that I see, is really known to me, if at all, only by inference from that percept.

Now it is not difficult to see what has gone wrong here. Russell has deployed, no doubt correctly enough, an account of the physical conditions in which seeing occurs, and in these has picked out as of crucial importance a certain event in the brain. He has then spoken of a 'percept' as either identical with, or perhaps as merely located in the same place as, this crucial cerebral event; and then instead of saying, perhaps defensibly, that the occurrence of a percept is a necessary condition of my seeing something, he has said, quite wrongly, that it actually is what I see. But *why* did he make just this mistake? What 'picture' was it that was here so powerfully at work?

This question too is not difficult to answer. It seems to be almost an occupational disease of those who reflect on the human nervous system that they should picture us as somehow located inside our own heads—at the point, that is, on which all the elaborate and ramified nerves converge. The observer is represented as being confined to the centre of his own nervous system, at a point from which as it were connecting wires run out into the outside world. In that world, it appears, there occur certain events which transmit electrical impulses along these wires, and thus there occur signals at the centre of the system, at the point where the observer is imprisoned and anxiously watching. Such signals, strictly speaking, are all that he ever observes. He may be able—it is not clear how —to form some dim notion of the remote, 'external' world; conceivably, by careful inference, he may reach conclusions as to its character which stand some chance of being true. But all that he really observes is the succession of signals arriving at the inside end of his nervous network; and these, of course, are all 'in his brain'.

I imagine that this way of representing the human predicament needs only to be clearly set out to be seen to be fantastical. Our nervous systems, so far from forming a barrier between ourselves and the 'external' world, in fact put us in touch (sometimes literally) with that world in the most direct of all possible ways; they are inside us, not we inside them. Nor need we now insist upon the numerous ways in which acceptance of this curious picture spells philosophical disaster. Our present concern is with its origin. Does it 'lie in our language'? If we allow it to drive us into flagrant absurdity, are we then deluded 'by means of language'?

Surely we are not. The bedevilling picture comes not out of language, but straight—or rather twisted—from the pages of textbooks on neurophysiology. The queer notion that what is seen must be in the brain certainly *results* in misinterpretation of 'our forms of language'; but it *derives* from misinterpretation, not of language, but of scientific discoveries. But why should they be misinterpreted in just this way? Why should the possession and use of a nervous system be disastrously compared, as in effect it thus is, with the possession and use of some sort of telephone exchange? This is not, we may think, hard to account for. The workings of a telephone exchange are comparatively familiar to all of us, and quite well understood; we all have a clear and tolerably accurate picture of the way in which such a system functions. Is it not then natural that the attempt should be made to understand, to explain, to render vivid and intelligible the comparatively *un*familiar workings of the nervous system by assimilating them, either overtly or by implication, to that other sort of system that we already picture quite clearly? To try to make something strange look more intelligible by representing it as like something already familiar is a device that, consciously or unconsciously, we all constantly employ, often with success. The temptation to bring the same device into play in cases where in fact it leads to disaster should surely be explained as owing, not to 'the bewitchment of our intelligence by means of language', but simply to the limitations of our intelligence. We do not always think clearly; and when we fail to do so problems may arise, some of which, as in the present case, are philosophical problems.

It will be observed that the present case has in fact the form of what Professor Ryle calls a 'dilemma'. In reflecting upon what we all ordinarily say and suppose about the use of our senses, and upon what the neurophysiologist says about his own closely related topics, Russell was led to think that there was a conflict between the neurophysiologist and the rest of us—that if what he had to say was true, as there was good reason to believe that it was, then much of what the rest of us say must surely be false. It is true that he seems not to have hesitated very long between this dilemma's horns, but rather to have impaled himself without further ado upon the horn of denying what we all know quite well to be true; still, the case was one of a dilemma in Ryle's sense. Now surely such dilemmas arise, or seem to arise, as a result of some failure in clarity of thought, some conceptual confusion.

That this may occur is merely an instance of human fallibility. Our liability to be led into confusion 'by means of language' is certainly *one* instance of our general liability to be misled; but it is *only* one; and even if there is reason to assign to this liability a pre-eminent role in the genesis of philosophical problems, there is no case, as I have tried to show, for representing this role as not only pre-eminent, but actually unique. In so far as Wittgenstein did this—and certainly he at least appears to have done it—he was surely mistaken. The aetiology of philosophy is more various than he suggested. Even if, to return to Ryle's words of 1931, we suppose that the task of philosophical analysis consists in exposure of or opposition to 'recurrent misconstructions and absurd theories'; even if we suppose that these show themselves in linguistic, that is, in conceptual, confusion; yet we should not assume that they all have their 'sources in linguistic idioms'. I do not believe that investigation of particular problems will support any such general theory as to their origins.

Chapter IX

SECOND RETROSPECT

How does the practice of 'analysis', as that was sketched in earlier chapters, now appear, if we look back from the point we have now arrived at?

Let us consider first the case of Moore. We have described him as being characteristically concerned to do two sorts of things—first, to insist that a number of ordinary propositions, or classes of propositions, which we all very often assert or believe, are *true*, and that those philosophers who have seemed or actually intended to deny them have shown no sufficient reason for doing so; and second, to clarify those and other propositions by formulating 'analyses' of them. He has been concerned, that is, both with the 'defence of common sense', and with that clarification of thought for want of which, as he believed, 'common sense' was often outraged and high metaphysical enterprises rendered abortive.

The first of these aims, certainly, is unexceptionable. It does not of course follow, from the fact that a proposition is very generally believed, that it is certainly true and ought to be defended. No doubt there are many quite ordinary propositions of the kind miscalled 'popular fallacies'—propositions, that is, both commonly believed and false. But none of the 'truisms' that Moore defended was of this character. None of them had any concern with any recondite evidence, or could conceivably have been overturned by any startling discovery. He was concerned with only the very simplest truths about ourselves, other people, and the world we live in—truths as to which we all certainly possess the best evidence there could be and far more of it than we need. It is certain that not a few philosophers have seemed to say, or have said, things incompatible with these impregnable truisms; and a resolute refusal to abandon them, or pretend to do so, is consequently by no means pointless.

However, it could be reasonably made a complaint that Moore tended to drop this sort of question at an unsatisfactorily early stage. It is all very well to point out that some philosopher has asserted what is fantastically untrue, or has denied what is both quite certainly true and very obvious. But surely the most interesting question which then arises is, *why* he should have done this. He is presumably neither insane nor brainless. There must surely be some explanation of his curious behaviour; and would it not be of very great interest to discover how his behaviour can be explained? But in this direction Moore did very little. He looked certainly for particular errors in particular cases; but he did not attempt, as Wittgenstein did, to get to the bottom of the whole peculiar business, to explain in some reasonably general way why blatant paradox should be so *characteristic* an outcome of philosophical argument. And this was serious, for it often gave to Moore's discussions an appearance of missing the point or of begging the question. He denied, rightly, the conclusions of some philosophical arguments. But so long as the arguments themselves were left unexamined, and the motives of those who so argued left undiagnosed, the forces productive of paradox were not effectively neutralized, and the paradoxical case not properly answered. It helps little to convince me that an assertion of mine is untrue, if I am still left with the conviction that there are reasons which compel me to make it.

The case of Moore's practice of 'analysis' is rather different. Here one might say that the methods he employed were not very well adapted to the end in view. The aim of analysis was to remove unclarity. Unclarity as to what? Not, in the ordinary sense, as to the meanings of words. We all know, and of course Moore knew that we know, what is meant by such a sentence as 'I see an ink-stand', or 'The author of *Waverley* was Scotch'. But although we all know well enough what such sentences mean, their 'depth grammar', as Wittgenstein calls it, is not at once obvious. The character of the concepts employed, their relations with other concepts, the various dimensions of presupposition and implication in their employment—all this is not obvious, and may give rise to perplexity. How then can we achieve 'a clear view' of these unobvious things? To look for an 'analysis' on Moore's pattern is to try to find some more explicit, less concentrated locution which will be logically equivalent to that to be analysed—will entail, be entailed by, and be independent of the very same things. But our language may well contain no such locution. And even if it does, can we safely suppose that to produce it will achieve all that is necessary? For at best we can clarify, by means of this sort of analysis, only the entailments, the narrowly logical features, of puzzling expressions; and may it not be that the source of perplexity lies quite outside this very limited area? To confine oneself to the pursuit of such analyses is in effect to concentrate upon, at best, only a small part of the use of our words and expressions; but the cause of our troubles may lie in our imperfect grasp of any feature of that use; there is, accordingly, no guarantee whatever that an 'analysis', even if it could be convincingly formulated, would alleviate our philosophical troubles. The most serious objection, then, to the programme of analysis is not that it is doubtful how far such analyses can be produced—though this is, in fact, quite a serious objection; it is rather that, even if they can be produced, they may well be philosophically unprofitable. What the case calls for, as one might put it, is not *definition* —not even, in Russell's phrase, definition 'in use'; it is by realistic *description of* use that we may hope to achieve that rational grasp of our concepts which disarms the philosophical tempter.

A good many of the same considerations apply, of course, to the programme of the Logical Atomists. But here the case is considerably complicated by the fact that they had, as Moore had not, a quite explicit mythology of language such that, if it had been true, it would have been reasonable to rely on the universal efficacy of 'analysis'. If our language had really been, as Russell thought it was, mere meat on the bones of a logical calculus; and if the calculus in question were,

I

as it actually was, quite simply and very rigidly
articulated, almost wholly independent of contextual
factors, and designed for the special field of fact-stating
discourse; then it *would* have been the case that most
of our ordinary expressions could have been properly
and even exhaustively analysed in the narrowly logical,
context-neglecting manner adopted by the practitioners
of 'logical analysis'. The essential task here, as Wittgenstein saw, was to bring out the extent to which this
notion of the character of language was a theorists'
fantasy—a case of seeming to see in the heavens a
pattern that is really marked out on the lens of the
telescope. Once this has been done, there is no longer
any *reason* to believe in the exclusive efficacy of old-
style orthodox analysis; and it can then be argued that
in fact it is *not* efficacious, on the lines already sketched
out in the discussion of Moore. This course is in fact
that which Wittgenstein himself had followed in his
process of self-conversion in the later 1920s.

In so far as the Positivists were also committed to
reliance on analysis of the orthodox pattern, much the
same considerations can be applied to their case: there
is no reason to suppose that the clarification of the
'vocabularies' of scientists and others, which they
professed as part of their objective, can be only or best
achieved in that particular way. For language is both
more flexible and more various than they, in this
following Russell, were accustomed to suppose. Their
hostility to metaphysics raises rather different questions. On this matter I believe it would now be most
effectively objected that, like Moore, they were

inclined to break off at too early a point. It is laid down
in effect by the Verification Principle that a (non-
analytic) proposition has meaning if and only if it can,
at least in principle, be verified. Suppose it to be
agreed that by 'verification' is meant here some kind of
empirical verification; and suppose further that the
utterances of metaphysicians are found or admitted to
be not susceptible of such verification. If so, then in the
terms of the Principle they have no meaning. But surely
the problem cannot well be left there? The Principle
provides indeed an excellently brusque procedure for
raising the question of the metaphysician's credentials,
and perhaps it may serve really to eliminate the grosser
sorts of philosophical nonsense. But in serious cases,
that deserve to be taken seriously, it hardly does more
than raise a question. To show that a certain metaphysical assertion is not a meaningful empirical statement is certainly to prompt the question, what then it
may be; but it does not answer this question. Even if it
were really the case, as in fact it is not, that non-
analytic indicative sentences could be significantly
employed only in making empirical statements—even
if, that is, the conclusion could really be drawn that the
metaphysician's employment of language was without
significance—it would still be a matter for serious
inquiry why this sort of deviation into nonsense should
occur so persistently. It is at just this point that Kant's
opposition to metaphysics had been much more
interesting and more effective. He had not attempted,
as the Positivists did, to explode the whole corpus of
metaphysics without troubling to wade through the

works of metaphysicians. He rightly felt that it was not enough to abuse their conclusions; their motives must be discerned and their arguments criticized, if any real grasp of the problems is to be achieved. It *may* be that in some sense the conclusions at which metaphysicians arrive are really without meaning; but if we are to be really rationally convinced that this is so, it is certainly necessary to examine the works in which, if anywhere, the meaning of their conclusions will be made clear. If one is so deeply unsympathetic to metaphysical argument that one cannot face this prospect, one would be well advised simply to leave metaphysics alone. Otherwise it will really be too easy to object that one is abusing what one has not attempted to understand. The Positivists too often exposed themselves to this objection.

It might perhaps be objected here that, however ill the brisk onslaughts of Logical Positivism may compare with the patient subtleties of Kant, at least it cannot, surely, be said that Kant's operations were more *effective*. For is it not evidently the case that the type of metaphysics against which those onslaughts were directed has, as nearly as may be, vanished from the philosophical scene? And what effect could be greater or more striking than that? But here there is a historical misunderstanding. The sort of supra-mundane, transcendent metaphysics which was the particular object of Positivistic odium was, in this country, already almost wholly extinct when their attack was launched. There was a coffin, perhaps, to be nailed up, but no Goliath to be conquered. The Positivists were already, as Kant in his day was not, on the winning side.

Two questions, I think, emerge with particular urgency from this brief retrospect. First, we shall have to consider, as was earlier foreseen, the question of the status of formal logic. For Russell it was the 'essence' of philosophy, at once the model of, and the means to, 'scientific' successes in philosophical inquiry. In as much as it revealed to us the 'essence' of language, its place in philosophical analysis must be no less essential. However, if language is not as this view requires that it should be, the case is altered; and we must try to see how. Second, since we have suggested that yesterday's hostility to metaphysics was at least not conclusively pressed home, we ought to give some consideration to the present position of that subject. Is it, as some have supposed, either likely or desirable that there should be a metaphysical revival? May it be that its recent and contemporary recession has been due to no more than a change of intellectual fashions, unimportant in the longer perspective of philosophical history? These are delicate questions, and perhaps it is perilous to meddle with them. However, it would not be quite honest to pass them by.

Chapter X

LOGIC

AT one point in his *Philosophical Investigations* Wittgenstein has the following passage: 'We see that what we call "sentence" and "language" have not the formal unity that I imagined, but are families of structures more or less related to one another.—But what becomes of logic now? Its rigour seems to be giving way here.—But in that case doesn't logic altogether disappear?'[1] We can scarcely suppose that logic *does* disappear. But the question which Wittgenstein asks is by no means an idle one.

'Symbolic Logic', Russell wrote in 1903, 'is essentially concerned with inference in general.' It investigates 'the general rules by which inferences are made'. He explains that the adjective 'symbolic' here indicates only the historical fact, theoretically irrelevant, that modern logicians employ in their writings various special non-verbal notations; 'symbolic' logic is, in principle, exactly the same as what has long been called 'formal' logic, the study of which is at least as old as Aristotle. One might expect Russell to add that the species of inference in question is *deductive* inference. He does not do this—only, however, for the curious reason that he denies that any genuine inferences are non-deductive. 'What is called

[1] op. cit., 108.

induction appears to me to be either disguised deduction or a mere method of making plausible guesses.' Thus we can say that, according to Russell, formal logic investigates the general rules by which deductive inferences are made, though he himself would have regarded the word 'deductive' as redundant. It is perhaps unnecessary to add that the subject is concerned not so much with rules by which inferences actually *are* made, as with rules which determine the validity or otherwise of inferences.

The concern of the logician is with *general* rules. What this means, or at least what it has always amounted to in practice, is that he concerns himself with such rules as are applicable in any subject-matter. The inference that, if all dogs are four-legged and all terriers are dogs, then all terriers are four-legged, happens to be about dogs; but its validity in no way depends on this. If the words 'dogs', 'terriers', and 'four-legged' were removed and replaced by other nouns and adjectives, the inference would still be a valid one. We can in fact put letters to mark the places where any such nouns and adjectives should go, thus: If all A's are B's and all C's are A's, then all C's are B's; and here we have an entirely general pattern of inference, valid in whatever subject-matter we choose. By contrast, 'all' could not be replaced by 'some', or 'most', or 'several'. The validity of this pattern of inference hinges essentially upon the force of the word 'all', though not at all upon the meanings of 'dog' or 'terrier'. We thus get a distinction between so-called 'logical constants', the irreplaceable words on

which the validity of general patterns of inference
depends, and items of non-logical vocabulary which can
be replaced by 'variables'—a contrast between such
general validity-determining words as 'all', 'some',
'if', 'and', 'or', 'not', and such particular-subject-
matter words as 'dog', 'blue', 'walk', 'evolution'. The
'general rules' which Russell mentions as the concern
of logic are such that they can be stated by the employment only of logical constants and variables.

Two questions now suggest themselves. First, how
does the logician decide what words to pick out as being
logical constants? And second, how does he decide
which patterns of inference in which they occur are
valid? The answers seem to spring naturally to mind.
First, it appears that we all already employ a number of
familiar, quite general, validity-determining words.
We already know, for instance, that from the proposition that Jones is in Birmingham *or* Manchester, one
cannot infer either that he is in Birmingham, or that he
is not, and furthermore that *any* inference of this
pattern would be invalid; but that, if the information
were added that Jones is *not* in Manchester, one
then could infer that he is in Birmingham, and any
inference of *this* pattern would be a valid one. The
word 'or' is thus manifestly a logical constant; and
similarly others could be identified in general use.
Second, as this example shows, we are all well able to
recognize good and bad inferences when we find them,
at least in simple cases; so that the logician's task
seems to be to discern and codify existing and well-
established practices. The general rules, then, which he

enunciates will evidently be a perhaps slightly trimmed and tidied version of rules actually recognized in our linguistic practice; and his constants will either be, or be symbolic analogues of, certain very familiar and ordinary words.

In the light of these considerations, one can perhaps feel something of the plausibility of the view which Russell took of his own work as a logician. He said of the calculus set forth in *Principia Mathematica* that 'it is a language which has only syntax and no vocabulary whatsoever. . . . It aims at being that sort of a language that, if you add a vocabulary, would be a logically perfect language.' It has no vocabulary, in that it is set out exclusively in terms of logical constants and variables. But if particular words of appropriate sorts replaced the variables and thus provided a vocabulary, it would then be a 'logically perfect' language in that the logical features of, and the logical relations between, its component sentences would be, as in ordinary talk they usually are not, both definite and clear. For the symbolism was devised to make overt and obvious what ordinary language too often veils and obscures. The calculus thus comes to be thought of as displaying the skeleton, so to speak, of ordinary language; conversely, language is seen as essentially this skeleton, but with flesh on its bones.

This view of logic, as we have seen, was incorporated into the very foundations of Logical Atomism. Atomic propositions were thought to have the form of the simplest formulae in such a calculus, and all other propositions to be derivable from them by applying the recognized rules of combination. Or, as Carnap expressed a part of this view some years later, 'In order to characterize a definite *language* it is necessary to give its *vocabulary* and *syntax*, i.e. the words which occur in it and the rules in accordance with which (1) sentences can be formed from those words, and (2) such sentences can be transformed into other sentences.'[1] It was supposed that the business of the logician was to lay bare the 'syntax' of our language, which thus, with the addition of its vocabulary, would be completely characterized.

Now it is clear enough that, if this picture were correct, language would have, in the words of our quotation from Wittgenstein, 'formal unity'. For the logician's calculus, which supposedly sets forth the 'syntax' of language, is, however complex it may appear, in fact systematically built up in accordance with comparatively few 'rules' out of extremely simple elements; and if language were indeed merely the flesh on these bones, it too would be fundamentally, though perhaps not obviously, simple, unified, and systematic.

There are, however, in fact innumerable points at which this rather pleasing picture of the state of affairs fails to fit the case as it actually is. We may begin by mentioning three very serious respects in which Carnap's recipe for the 'characterization' of a language is, when one comes to think of it, startlingly inadequate.

First of all, it is clear that the logician's interest in language is highly selective. In W. V. Quine's words, 'logic . . . has as its business the pursuit of truth'—'what

[1] *Unity of Science*, p. 38.

are true are certain *statements*. . . . The peculiarity of statements which sets them apart from other linguistic forms is that they admit of truth and falsity.' It is thus in language as a means of making statements, of saying things either true or false, that the logician is exclusively interested. (I do not say that this is necessarily so; but it has been so in fact.) But, as by now we scarcely need to be reminded, there are enormously many uses of language other than that of making statements. We use words to give orders, ask questions, express wishes, pass verdicts, to pray and to swear and to give undertakings. What we say in these uses cannot be assessed as being either true or false; so that these, and of course many other, uses of language do not come within the purview of the logician. Thus, the 'syntax' set forth in the logician's calculus could at best be the syntax only of a *part* of language. To imply otherwise would be to suggest that language has only one use, that of making statements; and though conceivably this might have been true, it manifestly *is* not true of any actual language.

Next we must take note of a grave complication as to sentence-formation. In the 'language' of, say, *Principia Mathematica* we find, as has been said, combinations of logical constants and variables. These variables are for convenience of different types—one sort is used, for instance, to identify places where predicates could be substituted, another sort to mark the proper places for subject-expressions. Rules can then be laid down by which formulae in the symbolism can be rejected as improper if the variables in them are wrongly

placed. Accordingly, in the process of 'adding a
vocabulary'—converting the formulae into actual sentences by putting words in the place of variables—
care must be taken to place the words appropriately;
nouns must not go where adjectives are required, nor
adjectives be substituted for subject-variables, and so
on. It is, however, obvious enough that, even if we
made no mistakes on this score, the resulting sentences
might often be perfectly meaningless. Such sentences
as 'Monday is square' or 'circularity is triangular'
have their subjects and predicates impeccably placed;
and yet they make no sense. It is clear, then, that if
'syntax' comprises only such rules as determine the
formation of formulae in a calculus, the specification of
syntax and vocabulary will not be enough, as Carnap
implied, to determine 'what sentences can be formed'
in a language. If meaningless sentences are to be ruled
out as *syntactically* wrong, then the syntax of any
language will have to be prodigiously elaborated in
indefinitely many dimensions.

Thirdly, there is another grave complication lurking
behind Carnap's allusion to 'the rules in accordance
with which . . . sentences can be transformed into
other sentences'. Such rules, he says, form part of the
'syntax' of a language. Now if the logician's concern
were really with *sentences*, this might perhaps stand
some chance of being true. But in fact, as Quine says,
his concern is with *statements*; for statements are, as
sentences are not, capable of being true or false.
And this fact is of the greatest importance. For
suppose that we raise, for example, the question

whether the statement that Jones is married can be 'transformed' into the statement that Jones is not unmarried. One might be inclined to say at once that it can be, simply in virtue of the 'syntactical' rule that double negation is equivalent to affirmation. But in fact the legitimacy of this transformation depends on at least two further assumptions—first, that the two statements be made at the same *time*; and second, that in both the same person be *referred to*. Now clearly there neither is nor could be anything in the *syntax* of a statement that would determine either when it was made, or about whom or what, if anything, it was made. And from this it follows that acquaintance with the syntax of a language could not possibly, by itself, be enough to enable us to decide what statements were legitimate 'transformations' of what others. It is, broadly, the relation of language to *context* which is ignored in discussion merely of the 'syntax' of language. But the fact is that, in most cases at least, unless a statement's 'contextual setting' is known we cannot even begin to consider its truth or falsity; we cannot indeed really *identify* a statement unless we know at least what it is about; but these things we cannot learn from any syntactical scrutiny.

We have found, then, three features of any actual language of which no account is taken by the constructors of logical calculi. First, there are a great many uses of language other than that on which they direct their attention. Second, there are restrictions upon the combination of words into significant sentences which are not, and indeed could not be, exhibited

in their 'syntactical' rules. And third, the whole
question of the relation of language to its context of use
eludes, again necessarily, the investigator of 'syntax'.
But a calculus, if offered as the picture of an actual
language, is not only incomplete in these ways; it is also,
in many other ways, an *idealization*. It is not only,
though of course this is true, that many words in any
actual language are vague, and hence often cannot be
fitted into any precise pattern of entailments. Their
uses are often, even though the words in question are
not vague, indeterminate in certain directions; and they
may of course also actually vary from time to time or
from one context to another. There are, again, in
almost any use of language *implications* of many quite
different kinds, and of varying degrees of inflexibility
—all, however, entirely different from the sharp, clear
relations that obtain between the formulae of a
calculus. A calculus thus is not an accurate picture
even of some few aspects of some part of language;
even if we rope off, so to speak, what it omits altogether, we are left with nothing so exact and relatively
uncomplicated as the firmly articulated formulae of the
logician. At best his calculi might be metaphorically
described as rather simple, conventionalized maps of a
language; they lack the fidelity of a detailed, realistic
aerial photograph.

To this state of affairs, which it would be tedious to
illustrate further, there are at least three possible re-
actions, which do not, though they might appear
to, exclude each other. One might, first, abandon the
general, over-ambitious idea of exhibiting in the form

of a calculus the logical skeleton of the *whole* of language, and adopt instead the less desperate objective of accurately mapping some restricted *part* of language. In this spirit it has been said by some logicians[1] that their aim is to display the anatomy of the 'language of science'—an area of language in which one might reasonably hope to find a tolerably high degree of precision, and from which inconveniently non-fact-stating locutions might be expected to be absent. Even here it would doubtless have to be admitted that any satisfactory 'schematization' would constitute in many respects a *revision* of the un-ideal actual practice of users of scientific language; however, it might be argued plausibly enough that a suitable calculus might be sufficiently like this particular department of language to be illuminatingly seen as a representation of it. Second, one might be inclined to abandon altogether any concern with any actual language, and to regard one's calculus as displaying the framework of a 'perfect' language—a perfect language being regarded not, as by Russell, as an undisguised, unveiled version of actual language, but simply as an ideal construction. This course has had many distinguished adherents; and though perhaps one might reasonably doubt what the ultimate purpose of such constructions could be, it could not be denied that the business of devising them has very considerable intrinsic interest. And third, it is possible to regard the calculi of logicians, not as accurate pictures of any

[1] See, for example, Quine, *From a Logical Point of View*, p. 106.

language or any part of language, nor as, so to speak, blue-prints for idealized constructions, but rather as interesting *derivations* from certain features of language —as exhibiting, in some ways the better by reason of their oversimplification, certain very fundamental features of any sort of discourse, which can be best examined, perhaps, in this unrealistic, highly abstract way. Rather similarly, a map may bring out some essential features of the ground all the better for being conventionalized, oversimplified, schematic, and incomplete; and it need not mislead one as to the character of the ground itself, provided that one does not rely on the map for any information other than that which it was designed to be capable of conveying.

It will be clear, I hope, that these ways of viewing the case do not exclude each other. For of course it may be simultaneously true of a given calculus that it provides a useful though very incomplete map of language in general, a fair approach to a detailed depiction of the language of science, and a (possibly) complete specification of the formal features of a specially invented language. It is thus quite unnecessary for those who prefer to look at the case in one way to conclude that those who prefer another way must be mistaken. What *would* be mistaken, however, would be to suppose that a specially invented language, incorporating exactly those features which some calculus allows for, is somehow enclosed within or buried beneath the surface multifariousness of our actual language. This is an illusion, and the cause of many other illusions; and it is most dangerous when combined, as in Logical

Atomism, with the metaphysical notion that reality too has its confusing surface, and, deeply concealed, its ultimate anatomy.

What, finally, of logic's apparent loss of 'rigour' as referred to in the question with which we began? The fact is, surely, that nothing has really lost any of its rigour. The logician's calculi, of course, have lost none. But ordinary language has lost none either; for *that* sort of rigour it has never possessed. If one imagined that a rubber doll contained a skeleton, one might well, on discovering the full range of its flexibility, conclude that its skeleton must have lost all of its rigidity. But if one possessed simply a rubber doll, and one then put beside it a skeleton of wire, no subsequent bendings of the doll would give just cause for suspicion that anything whatever had 'given way'. A calculus has as much precision and rigour as its inventors succeed in giving it; and certainly no damage is done to the rigour of logic by the discovery that a natural language has less.[1]

---

[1] This chapter has, as I am most clearly aware, made no more than a tiny scratch upon the surface of large and important questions. I would wish, therefore, strongly to recommend the reader to Mr. P. F. Strawson's *An Introduction to Logical Theory*, in which the problems at which I have glanced are very elegantly treated.

Chapter XI

METAPHYSICS

'PHILOSOPHY is many things and there is no formula to cover them all. But if I were asked to express in one single word what is its most essential feature I would unhesitatingly say: vision.'—'There is something visionary about great metaphysicians as if they had the power to see beyond the horizons of their time.'—'To say that metaphysics is nonsense *is* nonsense.'

These three quotations are taken from a recent article by Dr. F. Waismann.[1] They certainly indicate no disposition to regard metaphysics with contempt, as a pure waste of time, or as the product of some fundamental misunderstanding. To do this, he observes, would be to fail to acknowledge 'the enormous part played at least in the past by those systems'. We ought now to consider what part they did play—and also, why Dr. Waismann should have been inclined to put in those qualifying words, 'at least in the past'.

What, roughly at any rate, are we to understand by the notion of metaphysical 'vision'? Dr. Waismann writes that 'what is decisive is a new way of seeing and, what goes with it, the will to transform the whole intellectual scene. This is the real thing and everything else is subservient to it.' It is essential here, first of all, to distinguish carefully between a new way of

[1] *Contemporary British Philosophy*, Third Series, 1956, pp. 447-90.

seeing, and the seeing of something new. To see
something new, to find out what was not known before,
is not an exercise of *metaphysical* vision—even though
the effect of this new knowledge may even be to
'transform the whole intellectual scene'. It may be, for
example, that the theory of evolution has done as much
as anything in the last hundred years to alter our ways of
thinking, of seeing the world and our own place in it;
but this of course was a scientific and not a metaphysical theory, supported not so much by arguments
or would-be arguments as by an immense variety and
range of empirical facts. It is by contrast characteristic
of a metaphysical theory that facts should neither be
cited in its support nor be brought in evidence against
it; it was for this reason that the Positivists were able to
object that metaphysical doctrines were 'unverifiable';
such a theory consists not in an account of any new
facts but in a new account of familiar facts, a new
reading, so to speak, of what has already been agreed
upon.

But do not some *scientific* theories still come within
the scope of such a description? Certainly they do.
For example, the heliocentric theory of the planetary
system was of exactly this character. It offered a new
'way of seeing' astronomical phenomena without,
directly at any rate, adding to astronomical knowledge;
and no doubt it was for this very reason that it was
thought to be of far more than parochial significance—
to be, in fact, a revolutionary and even a dangerous
shift in the general intellectual landscape. However,
though such theories may often be felt to be of very

general, and therefore of some philosophical, importance, they themselves are certainly not metaphysical theories. Why not? Is it not because they are insufficiently general? The *direct* concern of the Copernican theory is solely with the movements of planets; its wider implications, if it really has any, are incidental. By contrast a metaphysical theory may be all-embracing, or immediately relevant at least to a very wide range of diverse phenomena. Such a theory as Spinoza's, for example, not only dictates a peculiar way of regarding facts in any field whatever; it was also at any rate intended to have precise moral and even religious consequences as well. It was intended to transform 'the *whole* intellectual scene', and to do this *directly*, not merely by implication, or in virtue of some quirk of psychology or association of ideas. And Hegel notoriously had no doubt whatever that there was a Hegelian way of seeing *any* subject-matter, however little in certain cases he may have succeeded in conveying to others what that way was.

'Suppose that a man revolts against accepted opinion, that he feels "cramped" in its categories; a time may come when he believes, rightly or wrongly, that he has freed himself of these notions; when he has that sense of sudden growth in looking back at the prejudices which held him captive; or a time when he believes, rightly or wrongly, that he has reached a vantage point from which things can be seen to be arranged in clean and orderly patterns while difficulties of long standing dissolve as though by magic.'[1] These words describe

[1] Waismann, loc. cit., p. 483.

exactly the situation of, for example, Berkeley. 'I wonder not', he wrote, 'at my sagacity in discovering the obvious tho' amazing truth, I rather wonder at my stupid inadvertency in not finding it out before.'[1] He had the sense, as he freely asserted, of 'a vast view of things soluble hereby'. It is worth looking into his case a little further.

Berkeley was familiar, mainly through Locke, with a 'way of seeing' the world that was chiefly derived from the thriving scientific inquiries of the seventeenth century. Material things were thought of as being atomic in structure, and in character predominantly mechanical. Our knowledge of them was supposed to be founded upon the occurrence in our minds of 'ideas' caused ultimately by the mechanical operation of 'corpuscles' upon our bodily organs; and it was thought to be at least an open question how far these ideas could be regarded as reliable indications of the actual character of the 'external' world. Fundamentally the physical world was thought of as a mechanical system, describable in quantitative laws, but known to us only 'indirectly', though the mediation of sensory ideas which in some respects almost certainly misled us as to the real character of our physical environment. By this way of seeing things Berkeley felt most violently 'cramped'. It appeared to him that the interposition of 'ideas' could end only in the sceptical overthrow of our claims to any actual knowledge of the physical world. He felt that the logical conclusion of the mechanistic view must be atheism, the idea that matter was God

[1] *Philosophical Commentaries*, 279.

or that there was no god at all. He could not see (and neither could Locke) how on this view the existence and immortality of the soul could be established. And in countless lesser details he thought that he found insoluble difficulties or undesirable conclusions. But then—and as it appears, quite suddenly—he came to see the whole situation differently. He changed, so to speak, his angle of vision. And at once all the problems seemed to disappear, to be replaced by a strange but startlingly simple new picture. Suppose that matter did not exist at all! What would be the advantages of this supposition? It would simply eliminate the problems of scepticism—for then there would be no 'external world' as to which we could wonder how far our 'ideas' corresponded with it. It would utterly deflate the pretensions of physical science, the 'corpuscular philosophy'—for there would be nothing for mechanistic hypotheses to be *true* of, they would have to be presented as, at best, convenient fictions to facilitate prediction. And what would be the disadvantages? None surely—for so long as we suppose 'ideas' to occur, the course of our actual experience would be exactly the same. And does it matter that there are no longer objects to cause these ideas? On the contrary—the notion that matter could be a true cause was in any case a bad one; and now the way is clear to attribute the occurrence of ideas to their proper origin, the will of God. On this view, then, scepticism is impossible; materialism is impossible; atheism is actually self-contradictory; so far from its being questionable whether the soul exists, there in fact exists *nothing* but 'spirits and ideas'. Is there not 'a vast view of things soluble hereby'? And so far from worrying over the fact that his new view has no ordinary, gross, experimental and factual consequences, Berkeley is particularly pleased to observe that from it Common Sense 'receives no manner of disturbance'. He believed indeed that his doctrine was capable of proof; but he never for a moment supposed it to be 'verifiable'.

Here, then, is a fair example of a metaphysical theory. Almost every paragraph that Berkeley wrote was intended to amplify, to defend, to explain, to render more acceptable the 'vision' of a theocentric, immaterial universe by which he had seemed able at one stroke to escape from the difficulties and horrors of Locke's scientific, 'corpuscular', material world. 'The arguments he will offer, the attacks he will make, the suggestions he will advance are all devised for one end: to win other people over to his own way of looking at things, to change the whole climate of opinion. . . . What is decisive is that he has seen things from a new angle of vision. Compared to that everything else is secondary.'[1] He is not like a man proving theorems or relating his discoveries; he is like a reformer endeavouring to propagate a cause.

Is there any value in such theories as these? Do such visionary projects of reform ever really succeed? It might be said that such theories may have, and often do have, the purely intrinsic value of admirable intellectual achievements; they speak well, as it were,

[1] Waismann, ibid.

for the capacities of the human mind; but do they ever make any actual difference? Sometimes they do—but seldom, it seems, quite the difference that their prophets intend. It appears to be most evidently true that, in its simple foundations, our ordinary 'way of seeing' the world is absolutely stable and obstinately unshakeable. Such a project as Berkeley's, which really requires us to abandon our notion of things as solid, substantial, enduring, indifferent to the presence or absence of percipient organisms, seems to attack our conceptual habits at so deep a level that it can really have no serious chance of succeeding. It is doubtful how far even Berkeley was able to retain the full sense of his vision for more than an occasional moment; one cannot so easily shake off what is natural to one's species. But we may, in other cases, come to see things differently in certain restricted fields—and really come to do so *naturally*, not in visionary moments only or in abstract theory. Dr. Waismann suggests that in the work of Descartes there may be 'a prophetic aspect of the comprehensibility of nature, a bold anticipation of what has been achieved in science at a much later date. The true successors of Descartes were those who translated the spirit of this philosophy into deeds, not Spinoza or Malebranche but Newton and the mathematical description of nature.' (Here Berkeley can be seen to have been working *against* the main trend of thought in his time.) And similarly the 'true successors' of Hegel might be said to be, not the philosophers who elaborated his doctrines into ever-deepening obscurity, but the historians whom he taught to find in the passage of time not merely a succession of independent episodes, but intelligible processes of change, of growth and decay, having certain analogies with the life-cycle of organic beings. Certainly there *may* be fields of inquiry, areas of knowledge, in which some metaphysician's new way of seeing may have the most fruitful and important results. But there may not be. His theory may stand as a mere eccentricity, with some interest perhaps, but no effect on anything whatever. Whether this will be so, he will doubtless be unable to foresee.

Why are there today few, if any, metaphysicians? The answer to this question, I believe, has at least three branches. First, there have never been many real metaphysicians at any time. To be, after all, sufficiently obsessed by a visionary project of intellectual reform to spend years upon its systematization and propagation is, fortunately no doubt, a very rare condition. There may well have been in earlier times a large number of *second-hand* metaphysicians, parasitic expositors of and elaborators on the theories of some truly original figure. But such secondary labours are surely as pointless as they are usually uninteresting. Of what interest would it be to patch up, to amend and expound, the doctrines of Bradley, if really one had no inclination whatever to share the queer view from which his own fervour was derived? It is reasonable enough to abstain from such work as this; for many vastly more interesting problems lie ready to hand. Is it really surprising that most philosophers should find in these other problems their best occupation? They are fortunate today in that so very many quite un-metaphysical problems have been brought into the light.

Second, it can, I think, be reasonably said that the conditon of true metaphysical fervour is today more difficult to achieve than was formerly the case; for it depends in large part upon a kind of illusion which, for good or ill and almost certainly for good, is now inevitably rare. Much admirable philosophical work has been done upon the notion of 'ways of seeing', of angles of vision, of—to speak more ponderously—alternative conceptual systems. We have become familiar enough with the idea that phenomena may be viewed in more than one way, comprehended within more than one theory, interpreted by more than one set of explanatory concepts. It has thus become almost impossible to believe that some *one* way of seeing, some *one* sort of theory, has any exclusive claim to be the *right* way; the notion of 'reality' itself, it would commonly be held, must be given its sense in terms of some particular theory or view, so that the claim that any such theory reveals or corresponds to 'reality' can be given a circular justification which is also open, in just the same way, to quite other views as well. But the belief that some new sort of theory is merely *possible*—that some novel set of concepts or categories *could* be employed—is hardly a sufficiently dynamic incentive to engender the production of a true metaphysical theory. If one has not, and one scarcely can have, the initial conviction that a novel 'way of seeing' has some *unique* claim to acceptance, one is unlikely to undertake the considerable labour of equipping it in a full metaphysical panoply. Such work is impossible perhaps, and certainly unattractive, to the disillusioned.

Finally, there are no doubt in our 'climate of thought' many factors of a more general kind that are in some way unfriendly to the metaphysical temperament. One might perhaps hazard the idea that metaphysical speculation has often arisen from, and often too been a substitute for, religious or theological doctrine. If so, it could be expected to show some decline in a period when very many people neither have, nor appear to be much oppressed by the want of, any serious religious convictions. It is not obvious that, if this were so, it ought to be deplored. It is, on the other hand, quite clear how undesirable it would be for philosophers to *pretend* to suffer from cosmic anxieties by which they were in fact not seriously troubled at all. Metaphysics, like religion, ought not to be manufactured in deference to any supposed requirements of intellectual decorum, or in the pursuit of some once genuine fervour which, in present conditions, would be synthetic or simulated.

Chapter XII

NEW QUESTIONS

IT might have been supposed, and in fact it was sometimes said, in response to the early impact of Wittgenstein's ideas that philosophy as he represented it was, at least theoretically, a suicidal subject. It would be broadly true to say that he was interested in liberating the mind from certain cramping, rigidifying prejudices, the characteristic effect of which was to distort the course of thought in certain fields, and to produce a characteristic sense of *impasse*, a kind of helpless intellectual discontent. Certainly the earlier history of philosophy provides an enormous mass of material for just this treatment; but the supply from this source, though very large, is finite. And for the future, might not the philosophical flies become themselves so wary and enlightened as not to go into the fly-bottle at all, and hence not to need the services of any liberator? If so, though no doubt the subject might still be pursued, would it not become in a way lifeless—an exercise, instructive perhaps but rather mechanical, in exposing old modes of confusion of thought by which hardly anyone continues to be seriously perplexed? Philosophy, if so, would have shrunk to the study of its own history, with perhaps some training in specially invented puzzles for educational purposes.

It is very possible, of course, that this state of affairs would not strike anyone but professional philosophers as undesirable. But in any case it is not at all likely to come about. For one thing, the hypothesis that all serious confusions should have been dissipated and no new ones encountered can safely be proscribed as Utopian; there is no near prospect of all, or even many, philosophical heads becoming flawlessly clear. More important, however, is the fact that there are now well established within philosophy a large number and variety of questions which are not parasitic upon prior confusion. My aim in this chapter is to indicate briefly what types of questions some of these are.

Among philosophers whose main work has been done in the last ten years, none has been more influential, or more original, than Professor J. L. Austin.[1] His manner of proceeding, which is characterized as a rule by a really astonishing minuteness and rigour, is not universally appealing, and it appears that to many its purpose is extremely obscure. However, though difficult to emulate, it is not, I believe, really hard to understand.

It is evident enough that at certain points Professor Austin's work is quite closely related to that of Wittgenstein. It was, as we have seen, an essential feature of Wittgenstein's practice to offer 'descriptions' of our uses of language—concrete, fully-realized examples or 'reminders' of those workings of language which, in philosophy, it is so easy and even natural to misunderstand and to misrepresent. In Professor Austin's work, too, the description of language certainly bulks

---

[1] His recent paper *A Plea for Excuses* (Proceedings of the Aristotelian Society, 1956-7) provides an excellent brief account and illustration of some of his aims and methods.

large. But a closer look reveals that, in the two cases, there are marked differences both of manner and motive. The difference of manner might be partly explained as follows. It would probably be true to say that Wittgenstein was interested, both by policy and by temperament, in large, or to use his own word, 'deep' conceptual distortions; and it seems reasonable enough to suppose that a large-scale, general distortion of thought could properly be attacked by means of a comparably broad and general description of language; large prejudices demand large missiles for their due destruction. In any case Wittgenstein's own descriptions were not, as a rule, protracted or very detailed or highly systematic; they took the form more often of hints, clues, and pointers than of set exposition. It might well be held, however, that not all philosophical tangles are of this deep, almost dramatic, character. Some, and those not necessarily the least important, may originate in comparatively slight distortions and misconceptions which, in the absence of very fully detailed inspection of our actual language, may either escape detection altogether, or at least not be seen in their full and fell significance. Furthermore, it could in any case well be held that the sort of description which will yield a really 'clear view' of something so complex as our uses of language must necessarily be lengthy and detailed. It is then, I think, partly for these reasons that a prominent feature of Professor Austin's procedure is the extreme detail in which he examines our language, and the sharpness of his eye and ear for very fine *nuances*.

But this difference of manner is more importantly connected, I believe, with a difference of motive. It was certainly held by Wittgenstein that description of language finds its whole *purpose* in the dissolution of antecedent philosophical problems; and hence, presumably, that it need not be further pursued than seems necessary if that purpose is to be achieved. Professor Austin frequently pursues this purpose also; but it is not the only purpose that he has in view. One might say that he believes that there is something to be *learned*, both *from* language and *about* language, which is worth learning whether or not we begin our researches in the grip of antecedent confusion.

In what sense, then, are there things to be learned from language? The point here is not, I think, a mysterious or difficult one. Suppose for example that we wish to investigate the notion of a person's *responsibility* for his actions; we wish to know what is contained, or how many different things are contained, within this notion. If we then consider the language used in discussing and assessing a man's responsibility for his actions, we find that the available vocabulary is surprisingly extensive. On the one hand are words like 'deliberately', 'intentionally', 'on purpose', 'knowingly', 'voluntarily'; and on the other are words like 'accidentally', 'by mistake', 'inadvertently', 'unwittingly', 'involuntarily', 'under duress'. Now it might be thought —and indeed it is often assumed without thinking— that this multiplicity of ordinary idioms is unimportant; that its interest is 'merely verbal', and that the important *general* question can be adequately discussed in terms of a simple contrast between, say, acting 'freely' and acting 'unfreely', or between 'voluntary' and 'involuntary' action. But to dismiss or ignore the wide variety of ordinary idioms as being 'merely verbal' is evidently to imply that it just *happens* (uninterestingly) to be the case that there is here a number of different ways of speaking, to imply that between them there are no significant differences. But it is surely enormously unlikely that this should be so. For language does not develop in a random or inexplicable fashion. It is to be *used* for a vast number of highly important purposes; and it is at the very least unlikely that it should contain either much more, or much less, than those purposes require. If so, the existence of a number of different ways of speaking is very likely indeed to be an indication that there is a number of different things to be said; it is an indication of genuine distinctions which, if they have called into being very commonly used expressions to mark them, are not at all likely to be unimportant. It is at the same time very *un*likely that any invented, artificial, or *ad hoc* terminology will be an improvement on that which has already satisfied the most stringent of tests—that is, survival in (probably) centuries of constant actual use. Rather similarly, it is certain that there is a great deal to be learned from the immensely various everyday idioms that we find in the vocabulary of sense-perception; and much *less* likely that we shall be greatly assisted by terms artificially introduced by philosophers.

Nothing excessive is here being claimed for our ordinary language. There undoubtedly exist some areas or topics of discourse in which our everyday idioms would be of very little interest indeed; in number-theory it does not matter in the least what ordinary uses there may be of the word 'number', and in zoology we can reasonably disregard the popular use of such words as 'animal' or 'fish'. There are certainly also some recondite problems for which no ordinary vocabulary exists and where neologism is not only justified but indispensable; psychology, for example, supplies a number of these. But where the topic at issue really is one that does constantly concern most people in some practical way—as for example perception, the ascription of responsibility, or the assessment of human character and conduct—then it is certain that everyday language is as it is for some extremely good reasons; its verbal variety is certain to provide clues to important distinctions; and it is *almost* certain to be more illuminating, to work much better, than any artificial, technical vocabulary would do. In such areas language is, as it were, a store-house of long-garnered principles and distinctions, enshrined there because they have been found important enough to merit specific linguistic recognition. If so, then on the one hand we override these distinctions at our peril; and on the other, if we wish to learn just what distinctions there are, it is to language that we can most hopefully turn for an answer. Thus, Professor Austin is concerned with our everyday language not merely, as Wittgenstein was mainly, because it serves to correct those prejudices which engender some philosophical problems, but also because it provides innumerable pointers to facts and

L

distinctions—which might, no doubt, be arrived at in quite other ways, but less certainly, and with much more labour. His aim is not merely to describe the workings of language, but also to learn from the description—to look through it, so to speak, at the facts about the world and our concern with the world which have moulded, and continue to mould, our ways of speaking. For this purpose the description must be exact and clear; for if it is not clear and true, it will not be transparent. Words reveal nothing if we do not see them as they are. We can learn from them only if we get to know them well.

I believe that it is now possible to throw some light also on a point at which, at first sight, Professor Austin and Wittgenstein appear to be totally opposed. It will be remembered that Wittgenstein dismissed the question 'How many kinds of sentence are there?' with the brusque observation 'There are *countless* kinds'. Professor Austin has sometimes appeared to oppose this directly—to hold that, though doubtless there are very *many* kinds, there is no reason why these kinds should not be classified and counted. But it is doubtful how far this apparent opposition is a genuine one. It is not certain that Wittgenstein meant exactly what he said. Certainly it is not clear in advance what constitutes a *kind* of sentences; and, as he says, new uses of language may sometimes crop up and others become obsolete. But equally it was not obvious in advance what should constitute a *kind* of animals; here too new kinds evolve and others die out; but we do not say simply that there are 'countless' kinds of animals;

we classify them, laboriously of course, as well as we can. What Wittgenstein probably had in mind was not quite that this *could* not be done for language, but that there would be no use in doing it; and by this he would have meant that it would not advance the treatment of the type of problems which engaged his own interest. This, though not certainly true, is at least arguable. But *this*, of course, is not quite what Professor Austin denies. He would probably, as a matter of fact, be inclined to hold that a really thorough and well-devised classification of 'kinds of sentence' *would* be of service even in dealing with Wittgenstein's favourite problems; but he would also, and perhaps with more confidence, hold that it would have great interest and value in itself, and would help us to learn much more from language more easily.

One purpose, certainly, which a system of classification may serve is that of *reminding* us, through acquaintance with its classificatory labels, of the variety of the phenomena within its field. It might be suggested that it is partly from the lack of any such reminder that philosophers, when they have discussed language, have concentrated overwhelmingly on just *one* kind of sentence, that, namely, in which statements are made. Against this obsessive preoccupation Professor Austin has launched a most powerful campaign. He has pointed out that even grammatically indicative sentences are by no means always used in making statements; that their utterance may be proper otherwise than by being true; and 'infelicitous' in countless ways other than that of

being false. He has devoted very great attention to
what he has called 'performative utterances', their
varieties and peculiar properties—utterances, frequently in the indicative mood, which have more of the
character of actions than statements, which are 'operative', by the making of which something is *done*.
This territory has proved to be remarkably fruitful,
and its exploitation powerfully disruptive of prejudices
about the working of language which had long been
almost instinctive in most philosophers, and damaging
even in their own over-favoured field of statements.
In Professor Austin's hands it provides a model, almost
a pilot-project, for a kind of inquiry into the realities
of speech and language which seems likely to be long
pursued and extensively developed. Nor is there any
doubt that a number of wholly traditional problems in
philosophy have been illuminated in the course of, or
as an effect of, this kind of inquiry.

This un-Wittgensteinian concern with classification
is to be found also in some of the work of P. F. Strawson, which in recent years has been of as much importance as any. He has been interested, however,
not so much in the invention of quite new modes of
classification, as in the attempt to make satisfactory
sense of some very ancient classificatory terms which
have long been neither valueless nor adequately clear.
He has investigated, with H. P. Grice, such centuries-
old topics as classification into 'categories', and that of
the distinction between 'particulars' and 'universals'.[1]
His readiness to do this suggests that he shares with

[1] *Proceedings of the Aristotelian Society*, 1953-4, pp. 233-60.

Austin the belief, contrary at least to the professions of Wittgenstein, that our language is not just *unlimitedly* various and diversified, completely Protean, entirely recalcitrant to general distinction and systematization; and that it is not, in certain fundamental respects at least, at all unstable. His own admirable, and indeed unique, work on the disputed frontiers between language and formal logic has led him, in fact, to raise certain very general questions about language which can be seen to arise quite naturally from, but do not at all resemble, philosophical questions as Wittgenstein conceived them.

It was one of the most paradoxical, but also most admired, contentions of Russell that very many ordinary propositions, which we should naturally regard as being of the subject-predicate form, are *really* not of that form at all. According to his celebrated 'theory of descriptions',[1] most such propositions must really be understood as existential statements. In his article 'On Referring',[2] Mr. Strawson first argued that this highly paradoxical doctrine could be seen to be unnecessary, if certain misconceptions were removed as to the use of expressions in referring to things. The motive for the paradox, that is, was to be removed by an accurate 'description' of that use of language which it misrepresented. A little later,[3] however, Mr. Strawson went further into the question

[1] See, for example, Russell, *Introduction to Mathematical Philosophy*, Chap. 16.   [2] *Mind*, July 1950. Also in *Essays in Conceptual Analysis*, ed. Flew, Macmillan, 1956.

[3] *Introduction to Logical Theory*, esp. pp. 184-90.

why this particular paradox should have been particularly seductive to a philosopher so much influenced by logic as Russell was; he argued that the very natural desire to assimilate language as closely as possible to a logician's calculus tended naturally to lead to neglect of 'referring' altogether, since in this use language is bound up with contextual factors in ways not paralleled in abstract calculi. However, some later logicians have argued that, though subject-predicate, 'referring' propositions admittedly *are* not, or cannot as Russell supposed be analysed as, existential statements, yet they can in theory be always eliminated and replaced by suitably framed existential statements.[1] If so, the close assimilation of language to calculi might still be practicable in theory; for the troublesome involvement with context of 'referring' expressions would be in principle needless and removable. Accordingly, there now arises the general question whether this recalcitrant feature of our language *is* in theory eliminable.[2] Must there be any singular referring expressions? Or is it, as is alleged, theoretically possible that all our purposes should be served by a language which contains no such use as 'referring'? It would not be in place here to attempt to answer this question. I have mentioned it, with some indication of how it has arisen, only as a specimen of a class of questions which are, so far at least as I can see, quite unlike any which Wittgenstein would have raised or been concerned with,

[1] See, e.g. Quine, *Methods of Logic*, p. 211.

[2] See Strawson, 'Singular Terms, Ontology, and Identity', *Mind*, October 1956.

and which are, though undoubtedly the proper business of philosophers, not 'philosophical' in the sense that he gave to that word. I hope that this example, and the others I have mentioned, may serve to show that we are not condemned to the sole task of correcting antecedent confusion. In philosophy, as in other subjects, there are certain points at which we are simply ignorant, and have knowledge to acquire; there are, as in other subjects, certain straight questions to which answers, with luck or by industry or both, may be discovered. This conviction, once no doubt over-confidently held, has been in some danger of abandonment through excessive reaction. It is a matter of some importance that it should be re-established.

Against the investigations of Professor Austin it is sometimes objected either that they are unimportant, or that they are not philosophical, or both. (Mr. Strawson, whose inquiries have almost always at least begun from some active philosophical storm-centre, is probably less often beset by these objections; but even in his case attention to uncustomary points, or uncustomarily perceptive attention to familiar points, has been found to cause protest among the hasty or the very conservative.) With the charge of unimportance it is of course difficult to deal, since it is seldom made clear by what sort of standard importance is here to be assessed. Furthermore, such questions are not easy to discuss without acrimony. The notion that Professor Austin's inquiries do not deserve to be called 'philosophical' is, however, rather more interesting. It would of course be easy to say that it does not matter in the least what his inquiries are to be called; if some do not wish to apply to them the name of philosophy, let them by all means refrain from applying that name. But it is not, I think, at all necessary to take this short way with the question, since the employment of the name 'philosophy' can quite easily be defended.

It would, I imagine, now be generally agreed that the proper concern of philosophy is with concepts, with the ways in which and the means by which we think and communicate. It would also be generally agreed, for very obvious reasons, that this implies a concern with the uses of words. In the history of philosophy we find ourselves confronted, not of course exclusively, but still very frequently, with certain crucial and usually recurrent conceptual difficulties, showing themselves in, and perhaps often generated by, misconstructions or misuses or both of certain words and expressions. It is admittedly a philosophical task to understand, to correct, and thereafter if possible to avoid, these misconstructions and misuses and their attendant perplexities. On this point, I believe, there would be no disagreement. Why then, one may ask, should this negative, or curative, procedure not lead on to the positive investigation of the actual, non-distorted, non-misconstrued uses of the expressions concerned, and indeed of others? It is certainly a matter of importance to expose and to avoid the conceptual knots which have been tied in the course of centuries of philosophical argument. Why should one not then begin on the acquisition of systematic conceptual knowledge? We are for the most part extremely unclear both *what* our concepts are, and *why* they should be as they are. There is here a great deal to be found out and, if possible, explained. To hold that such investigations ought not to be undertaken, or that, if they are undertaken, they should not be called philosophy, is like maintaining that, for instance, non-clinical psychology is either a waste of time, or not really psychology. It is certainly important that attention should be devoted to relieving the psychological afflictions that occur in abnormal cases; but it would be most singular to maintain that, *unless* the relief of some affliction is the object in view, psychological research should be either not undertaken or at least renamed. One might venture indeed to continue this analogy. If psychotherapy were never to be supported by any corpus of non-clinical psychological knowledge, one would perhaps expect it to remain in a rather unhappy, jumbled, improvised, and *ad hoc* condition: if the delineation of concepts for the purpose of dispelling perplexity were never to be backed by any more detailed and systematic conceptual researches, one might well expect such delineation as occurred to be somewhat fragmentary and inadequate

But in fact there is no need to 'expect' this; the case is before us.

Chapter XIII

PHILOSOPHY AND BELIEF

PHILOSOPHY in the last fifty years has often been said, both by its friends and its enemies, to have undergone a 'revolution'. The questions in what this so-called revolution has consisted, what have been its effects, and whether those effects are to be lamented or not, have been widely discussed and almost inextricably confused. A few final words here will not do much, but may do something, to sort things out.

The two observations most commonly made by way of picking out the novelty in contemporary philosophy are probably, first, that it is now 'anti-metaphysical', and second, that it has become entirely 'linguistic'.

On the first of these points not much needs now to be said. It could not well support, I believe, the claim (or accusation) that a 'revolution' has occurred. For one thing, although philosophy at present is for the most part admittedly *un*metaphysical, it is not doctrinally *anti*-metaphysical in the manner of Logical Positivism; and further, as I tried to show at the beginning of this book, metaphysical writing in the style of Absolute Idealism has itself no just historical claim to the status of a tradition or an orthodoxy. Russell and Moore were not wholly pursuing revolutionary new paths; they could almost as well be represented as reverting to old ones. The manner of Russell or of Professor Ayer is indeed strikingly unlike

that of Bosanquet or Bradley; but it is related nearly
enough to that of Mill or Hume. If what is complained
of is the absence of high-flying metaphysical eloquence,
then this is a complaint which could have been made of
British philosophy a hundred and fifty years ago as
well as today. There is here, then, no solid basis for
talk of 'revolution'.

More interest, however, attaches to the proposition
that contemporary philosophy has become 'linguistic'.
There are some who maintain that this is simply not
true, or at least that to assent to the description
of philosophy as linguistic is both misleading and
strategically imprudent. Sir Isaiah Berlin has said
that contemporary philosophers 'have done themselves
unnecessary harm, in the eyes of the uninstructed, by
advertising their methods as "linguistic". No doubt
this was a tempting and perhaps necessary weapon in
the early days, when the current philosophical jargon—
and the vast inflation of language by Hegelians and
their allies—needed a sharp and immediate antidote. . . .
But of course what philosophers are talking about is
not words *qua* words, but about concepts and categories: the most general and pervasive among them
which particular uses of words constitute (for thought
is largely a matter of using words). Words are not
distinguishable from the concepts they express or
involve: but it does not follow that all there is before
us is "mere words"—trivial questions of local usage.'[1]
However, this objection to the description of current
philosophy as 'linguistic' seems to amount to no more

[1] *The Twentieth Century*, June 1955, pp. 508-10.

than that 'the uninstructed' may be led by that description to think ill of the subject, through drawing from it a conclusion which in fact 'does not follow'. And a desire to save the uninstructed from the consequences of their own fallacious reasoning seems hardly a sufficient motive for rejecting a description which in some sense at least is quite clearly correct. It may be true that philosophers do not as a rule talk about words '*qua* words'; but they do very often talk about words; and that they do so is certainly the most immediately obvious difference between their work and that of their predecessors. The use of the term 'linguistic' may have been 'unfortunate'; but it is also accurate enough and, one might add, candid.

But of course it is not, by itself, very informative. What is of importance after all is not the bare fact that words have come to be much discussed by philosophers, but the reason for which this has come to be so. This reason lies in new views as to the nature of the subject. Briefly, it has come to be realized more clearly than ever before (unless perhaps by Kant) that philosophical questions, if indeed there are any such questions, must be somehow distinguished on the one hand from questions of empirical fact, and on the other hand from formal (mathematical, logical) questions. Such questions do not arise through ignorance of fact, nor are they to be answered by deductive calculation. They arise at points where we do not 'command a clear view' of our 'concepts and categories', where in a sense we do not even see quite what the question is or, hence, how it should be approached. They may be the expression of simple perplexity—of 'the form: I don't know my way about'. They may express, more sharply, the sense of an evident 'dilemma'. Or they may give expression to a disinterested curiosity about the frequently unobvious features, whether detailed or very general, of the concepts we employ. But in all cases light is to be found, if it can be found, from a grasp of our concepts, of 'the ways in which we think and communicate'.[1] And of course, since we think and communicate predominantly in words, it follows that the uses of words must be a main topic of inquiry. That this is so does not indicate that philosophers today are concerned (though to *some* extent they are concerned) with questions quite different from those which preoccupied their predecessors; it is the effect of a new and a manifestly beneficial awareness of the character which most 'philosophical' questions have always had. It is in this respect that, in Berlin's words, 'there *has* been a great (and I should say, beneficent) revolution'. The effect of it has been to throw into new prominence discussion, not quite of the words we use, but of the ways in which we use them. And I see no good reason, if this is made clear, for much objecting to the label 'linguistic' as a mark of change.

There remains, however, a matter for controversy. There is a peculiar sense of the noun 'belief' which, for want of any ready means in English of making it intelligible, is often supplied with some sort of explanation by reference to the word *Weltanschauung*.

[1] Berlin, loc. cit., p. 510.

It may be thought, and it is, in its turn unclear what this word means. Nevertheless, the questions whether philosophy has, or should have, had at one time or ought to have had, direct relevance to questions of 'belief' in this peculiar sense have been widely canvassed, and most variously answered. They deserve some attention.

I am in fact inclined to think that, when one comes to look into these questions at all closely, they either break up or melt away to such a degree that any general statement becomes quite impossible. Let us turn first to the historical question. It may be true, in Dr. Waismann's words, that 'at the heart of any philosophy worth the name is vision'. Put otherwise, there is almost always to be found in the work of eminent philosophers of the past a characteristic 'way of seeing' such that, if in any given case one can come to understand what this typical way of seeing was, then a certain order, coherence, and intelligibility can be observed in and perhaps throughout the work of that philosopher. It could very well be argued that some such dominating vision, some characteristic way of looking at things, has been found to be a necessary condition of long-run philosophical survival. But such visions have both been, and been thought to be, exceedingly various both in their implications and in their own characters. They may, as in the case of Spinoza, be thought to entail particular religious and moral consequences; they may bear, as with Berkeley, on religion but scarcely if at all on morality; or as with Hume, on morality perhaps but on religion not at all. They may be in themselves extraordinary, as in

Bradley's case, or comparatively humdrum as in the case of Locke. They may derive, as with Hobbes and many others, from natural science; with Berkeley again, from opposition to science; with Descartes, from mathematics; with Russell, from logic: and in different cases the relation or relations between the 'vision' and ordinary opinions, or religion, or politics, or ethics, or aesthetics may either be, or be thought to be, or both, either intimate or remote or non-existent. To say generally, in fact, that philosophers before the present century were directly or closely concerned with questions of 'belief' becomes quite impossible, as soon as any particular belief or kind of belief is mentioned. Were they all concerned with or was their work particularly relevant to questions of religion? Certainly not. To questions of morality? In some cases only. To political questions? Comparatively seldom. Some 'vision' or other perhaps they all had. But what those visions had to do with general, non-technical issues of 'belief' is a question which cannot possibly be answered except in particular cases. The facts are too various for any quick summary.

It is, however, entirely clear that concern with very general questions of religious or moral or political belief has at no time either been or been thought to be *peculiar* to philosophers, even if the work of some philosophers, rightly or wrongly, has been adjudged to be *relevant* to such questions. There has never been any dearth of direct, non-philosophical religious, moral, and political writing. Occasionally the work of scientists has been powerfully, though doubtless indirectly, effective in these fields. And not a few novelists, dramatists, and other such persons have made matters of 'belief' their fundamental concern. Indeed there is not, I believe, any serious doubt that among the many forces which tend to shape and modify the prevailing beliefs and attitudes of societies, the influence of philosophers has been on the whole exceedingly small, and on any view is certain to remain so. Philosophers are less numerous than the clergy, less intelligible than novelists, less exciting than political pamphleteers, less revered than scientists. A philosopher who leaves the beliefs of the public alone need not fear that those questions will cease to be pursued and publicized, nor perhaps could he hope for much success if he should enter that arena. It may be in part for this reason that even those philosophers who berate the ideological neutrality of their colleagues do not themselves seem eager to tell us what we should believe, or how we should live.

I hope it may be remembered, then, that the relation of earlier philosophy to questions of *Weltanschauung* is a matter so ramified and complex that hardly anything of a very general sort can usefully be said about it. If so, this puts a large obstacle in the way of debating the question whether in this respect contemporary philosophy has changed. For what *is* this respect? Exactly what is the situation from which, if philosophy has changed, it is to be said to have departed? There really exists no antecedent position sufficiently simple and stable for philosophy today to be assessed, in relation to that position, as the same or different.

However, it is possible to venture one or two remarks, vague though the question is on which they may be supposed to bear.

It is at any rate certain that questions of 'belief'—questions of a religious, moral, political, or generally 'cosmic' variety—are seldom if at all directly dealt with in contemporary philosophy. Why is this so? The first part of an answer to this question can easily be given: there is a very large number of questions, not of that variety, which philosophers find themselves to be more interested in discussing. But many would go further. They would wish to say that philosophy has nothing to do with questions of *that* kind. Political philosophy involves the study of political concepts, but says nothing of the rights or wrongs of political issues. The moral philosopher examines the 'language of morals', but does not as such express moral judgements. The philosopher of religion may be, but by no means need be, a religious believer. They would say, more generally, that philosophy is the study of the concepts that we employ, and not of the facts, phenomena, cases, or events to which those concepts might be or are applied. To investigate the latter is to raise political or moral or religious, but not philosophical, problems or questions. It will be seen that this view is closely related to the Positivistic thesis that philosophical problems are 'syntactical', 'formal' rather than 'material'—a thesis which most would now hold to have been too narrowly formulated, but with the spirit of which a great many would be in sympathy.

From this attitude two questions may arise that

M

should be carefully distinguished. It might be objected, first, that matters of 'belief', though indeed quite distinct from the problems now classed as philosophical, ought *also* to be made, at least more frequently, subjects of discussion among philosophers. To say simply that these matters are no part of philosophy is, it might be held, to impose an arbitrary and unreasonable restriction upon the scope of the subject, a restriction, moreover, for which there is no historical warrant. Are there not questions of a quite non-technical sort, questions about life in general and attitudes to life, which historically have been at any rate touched on by most philosophers, and which furthermore are vastly more interesting to people in general than are the highly abstract, highly 'professional', and frequently minute disputations in which philosophers currently engage?

This is not, I believe, an impressive point. No doubt one would not wish to deny that there are very vital and interesting questions of this sort. But does it follow that philosophers ought to discuss them? Have they not perhaps, like physicists or philologists, their own special and specialized concerns in which in fact, for what the point is worth, they are evidently more interested? Is it really any use exhorting or instructing them to do something else? Their position after all is not usually such that they have any great interest in pleasing the public or pursuing mass audiences; they would not be much put out if those whom their work did not attract should pay simply no further attention to it. Even if, as in fact is not perfectly clear, their present concerns are somewhat more confined than the concerns of philosophers historically have been, it is not clearly improper nor in the least degree unusual for such progressive specialization to occur. Finally, is it certain that those philosophers who have dealt largely in *Weltanschauung* have done so to any great purpose or profit? And could it be any more certain that, if those questions were now to be more frequently mooted among philosophers, the outcome would be particularly valuable? A marked capacity for abstract thought is compatible with an 'attitude to life' entirely ordinary, or even dull. A philosopher's views in this area might be expected to be consistent and reasonably clear; but they might well, while fulfilling those conditions, be absolutely uninteresting. If so, one need not complain if he should keep them to himself.

But second, some philosophers, conscious perhaps of the lack of weight in this first objection, have raised a rather similar point in a more telling form. The view that philosophy is, to repeat an expression employed just now, ideologically neutral is held widely enough for it to be becoming increasingly fashionable to deny it. The fashionable objection is that current philosophical views and procedures are *not* distinct from, unrelated to, matters of the *Weltanschauung* variety; so that for philosophers to disclaim any concern with those matters amounts in fact to their being blind to the implications of their practices. The suggestion is not that questions of a different kind should be admitted within the scope of philosophy, but that those questions necessarily are within its scope already and therefore ought not to be, as they often are, passed over in silence. Discussion of this important suggestion has suffered, unfortunately, from extreme imprecision. Points have been made on either side of extreme generality and quite indeterminate effect. It has been said in support of the suggestion, truly enough, that some religious and even some political authorities have seen in contemporary philosophy implications sufficiently grave and substantial to merit suspicion or open hostility; could this be so, if the subject were ideologically neutral? But to this it can easily be replied that those authorities have perhaps not understood the character of their adversary; may they not be oppressed by implications which are not really there? It may then be urged on the other side that philosophers themselves actually exhibit a quite striking ideological range— politically from left to right, in religion from Roman Catholicism to atheism, in morality from puritanism to marked un-rigour; yet broadly the same sort of philosophical practice appears to be compatible with any of these positions. To this in turn it can be not absurdly replied that perhaps, underlying these apparent gross differences, there may be some deep-seated similarity of attitude and outlook, in which it may be that future historians will find without difficulty the *Weltanschauung* of contemporary philosophy. What is certainly lacking is any *demonstration* of the ways, if any, in which current philosophy has such general implications, to set against the undeniably plausible *prima facie* contention that it has none.

However, this might be attributed to the difficulty of becoming aware, at any given time, of the deepest, most unquestioned presuppositions of the day. If so, it would appear to be the course of prudence to await with due humility the verdict of history.

It is in any case a rather curious fact that philosophy in general should be made so often a target for public complaint or criticism. There are after all a great many academic subjects in which, as they are at present pursued, the general public neither finds nor could well be expected to find any sort of interest. Yet no one is moved to complain of this state of affairs, or to urge the professors of those subjects to turn their hands to matters that would engage the concern of a wider audience. Why are philosophers not thus allowed to go their own way? No doubt there are many reasons. But one, I think, is this. There is a sense in which philosophy has only rather recently achieved professional status. This has occurred in two ways. First, 'where Mill, Huxley, and Leslie Stephen had published their articles in the ordinary reviews, Bradley, Moore, and Russell published theirs in the philosophers' professional organ or in the Proceedings of the philosophers' metropolitan forum. This new professional practice of submitting problems and arguments to the expert criticism of fellow craftsmen led to a growing concern with questions of philosophical technique and a growing passion for ratiocinative rigour. Eloquence will not silence rival experts and edification is not palatable to colleagues. . . . Philosophers had now to be philosophers' philosophers; and in their colloquia there was as little room for party politics as there is in courts of law.'[1] Second, it is only quite recently that the subject-matter, or rather the tasks, of philosophy have come to be clearly distinguished from those of other disciplines. In this way too, connected of course with the other, the subject has not long been standing firmly on its own feet in its own territory. For these reasons I believe that philosophy has not yet been accepted as a subject which its practitioners should be left to practice. There lingers a certain sense of the old, kind days of amateurism, the days, as it were, when anyone could join in, could have his own say, and could expect to be listened to. Those who have not moved into, or have moved out of, professional circles have, perhaps, still a sense of a certain deprivation, a vague feeling that the total amateur ought not to be disqualified from engaging in what was, so recently, an amateurish pursuit. (I believe that the position of literary criticism is here very similar.) On the professional side too there is perhaps a certain nostalgia. The old amateurs were occasionally conspicuous public men. Their cogitations were of interest to, and rightly or wrongly were thought to be of importance in, far wider circles than would now be likely to be reached by even the most admirable of contributions to philosophy. Thus, perhaps, it comes about that certain philosophers deplore the present aspect of their own subject, and that, more commonly, certain non-philosophers discuss philosophy with a plaintive and patronizing impertinence which they would not dream

[1] Ryle, *The Revolution in Philosophy*, Introduction, p. 4.

of displaying towards any other subject in which they were admittedly ill qualified. There is not much need to worry about this. The present state of affairs is doubtless temporary and transitional; and in the meantime the complaints that are made are quite certain to be ineffective.

For my own part I am inclined to think that they only need feel strongly hostile to contemporary philosophy who have cause to fear or to dislike a clear intellectual air and a low temperature of argument. It seems to be true that the contemporary philosopher's eye is characteristically cold and his pen, perhaps, apt to be employed as an instrument of deflation. It is largely for this reason that, however narrowly technical, however refined and minute and even pedantic, the pursuits of philosophers may be or may become, any age or society in which those pursuits were wholly neglected would be, in my judgement, seriously the worse for that. In our own case we have, at present, no ground for apprehension.

SHORT BIBLIOGRAPHY

I HAVE included in the following list, apart from some of the more important writings of philosophers discussed or mentioned in the text, a small number of other books and articles which seem to me to be either valuable in themselves, or representative of the periods in which they were written, or both.

I. Books:

G. E. MOORE, *Philosophical Studies*, Kegan Paul, London, 1922.

—— *Some Main Problems of Philosophy*, Allen and Unwin, London, 1953.

BERTRAND RUSSELL, *The Problems of Philosophy*, Home University Library, 1912.

—— *Our Knowledge of the External World*, Allen and Unwin, London, 1914.

—— *Mysticism and Logic* and other essays, Longmans, London, 1918.

—— *Introduction to Mathematical Philosophy*, Allen and Unwin, London, 1919.

—— *The Analysis of Mind*, Allen and Unwin, London, 1921.

—— *An Inquiry into Meaning and Truth*, Allen and Unwin, London, 1940.

—— *Logic and Knowledge*, Allen and Unwin, 1956.

C. K. OGDEN and I. A. RICHARDS, *The Meaning of Meaning*, Kegan Paul, London, 1923.

C. D. BROAD, *Scientific Thought*, Kegan Paul, London, 1923.

C. I. LEWIS, *Mind and the World Order*, Scribner, New
York, 1929.

F. P. RAMSEY, *The Foundations of Mathematics* and
other logical essays, Kegan Paul, London, 1931.

R. CARNAP, *The Logical Syntax of Language*, Kegan
Paul, London, 1937.

L. WITTGENSTEIN, *Tractatus Logico-Philosophicus*, Kegan
Paul, London, 1922.

—— *Philosophical Investigations*, Blackwell, Oxford,
1953.

—— *Remarks on the Foundations of Mathematics*,
Blackwell, Oxford, 1956.

G. RYLE, *The Concept of Mind*, Hutchinson, London,
1949.

—— *Dilemmas*, Cambridge University Press, 1953.

H. H. PRICE, *Thinking and Experience*, Hutchinson,
London, 1953.

A. J. AYER, *Language, Truth, and Logic*, Gollancz,
London, 1936; 2nd edition, 1946.

—— *The Foundations of Empirical Knowledge*, Macmillan, London, 1940.

—— *Philosophical Essays*, Macmillan, London, 1954.

—— *The Problem of Knowledge*, Macmillan, London,
1956; also in the Pelican Philosophy Series.

JOHN WISDOM, *Other Minds*, Blackwell, Oxford, 1952.

—— *Philosophy and Psychoanalysis*, Blackwell, Oxford,
1953.

P. F. STRAWSON, *An Introduction to Logical Theory*,
Methuen, London, 1952.

W. V. QUINE, *From a Logical Point of View*, Harvard
University Press, 1953.

II. Collections

In the following books are brought together a number of valuable articles, many of which it would have been necessary to mention separately if they had not been thus conveniently assembled. Some are reprintings of articles originally published elsewhere; but many were specially written for the collections in which they appear.

Readings in Philosophical Analysis, ed. Feigl and Sellars, Appleton-Century-Crofts, 1949.

Philosophical Analysis, ed. Max Black, Cornell University Press, 1950.

Logic and Language, First Series, ed. Flew, Blackwell, Oxford, 1952.

Logic and Language, Second Series, ed. Flew, Blackwell, Oxford, 1953.

Essays in Conceptual Analysis, ed. Flew, Macmillan, London, 1956.

Contemporary British Philosophy, Third Series, ed. Lewis, Allen and Unwin, London, 1956.

The following two volumes are mostly about, but in part also by, the philosophers indicated:

The Philosophy of G. E. Moore, ed. Schilpp. Northwestern University, 1942.

The Philosophy of Bertrand Russell, ed. Schilpp. Northwestern University, 1946.

The Revolution in Philosophy (Macmillan, 1956) consists mostly of broadcast talks on recent philosophy. The Introduction is by Professor Ryle.

III. Articles

I mention here a few recent articles which have not been reprinted in any other form.

SUSAN STEBBING, 'The Method of Analysis in Metaphysics', *Proceedings of the Aristotelian Society*, 1932-3.

A. J. AYER, 'Verification and Experience', *Proceedings of the Aristotelian Society*, 1936-7.

—— 'Does Philosophy Analyse Common-Sense?', *Aristotelian Society Supplementary Volume XVI* (1938).

P. H. NOWELL SMITH, 'Philosophical Theories', *Proceedings of the Aristotelian Society*, 1947-8.

I. BERLIN, 'Logical Translation', *Proceedings of the Aristotelian Society*, 1949-50.

F. WAISMANN, 'Synthetic-Analytic', *Analysis*, 1950 ff.

H. L. A. HART, 'A Logician's Fairy Tale', *Philosophical Review*, 1951.

G. E. MOORE, 'Wittgenstein's Lectures in 1930-33,' *Mind*, 1954-5.

P. F. STRAWSON, discussion of Wittgenstein's 'Investigations', *Mind*, 1954.

N. MALCOLM, discussion of Wittgenstein's 'Investigations', *Philosophical Review*, 1954.

J. L. AUSTIN, 'How to Talk', *Proceedings of the Aristotelian Society*, 1952-3.

—— 'A Plea for Excuses', *Proceedings of the Aristotelian Society*, 1956-7.

P. F. STRAWSON, 'Particular and General', *Proceedings of the Aristotelian Society*, 1953-4.

—— 'Singular Terms, Ontology, and Identity', *Mind*, 1956.

SUPPLEMENT TO BIBLIOGRAPHY
(1961)

OF books first published since this book was written two in particular should be mentioned—Professor Stuart Hampshire's *Thought and Action* (London, 1959) and Mr. P. F. Strawson's *Individuals: an Essay in Descriptive Metaphysics* (London, 1959). Just before his death in 1958 G. E. Moore had prepared for publication a collection of *Philosophical Papers* (London, 1959).

A Hundred Years of Philosophy, by John Passmore (London, 1957) is an excellent historical study, and deals with the period covered in this book much more comprehensively than could have been attempted here.

INDEX